CAPTAIN
DESMOND ELLIS HUBBLE

ROYAL ARTILLERY, SPECIAL OPERATIONS EXECUTIVE

BY

MICK MANISE

Grosvenor House
Publishing Limited

This book is published by
Grosvenor House Publishing Ltd
28-30 High Street, Guildford, Surrey, GU1 3EL.
www.grosvenorhousepublishing.co.uk

A CIP record for this book
is available from the British Library

ISBN 978-1-78148-958-1

Dedicated to all those of the generation who sacrificed so much in order that my children and I could be born and live our lives in times of freedom and safety.

INTRODUCTION

In June 2005 my wife Christine and I were on a motorcycling holiday in France where I was indulging my passion for history on the Normandy Beaches, the Somme and a special personal trip to the Ardennes region where I was aware that there was a forest and a river bearing the name Manise. I had always wondered why this was the case and was aware that my great grandfather was born and bred there but emigrated to live in London in 1896.

On the outskirts of a town called Revin, near to the Fôret de la Manises, we found a stone memorial commemorating the martyrs of the Maquis des Manises and the events of 13th June 1944. Whilst taking photographs for future research, I noticed a name through my view finder which made me look up and wonder why it was there. The names of over a hundred men from 17 years and older were carved into the memorial but the name that stood out did so because it was English, Desmond Ellis Hubble. The obvious choices were that he must have been either downed allied aircrew in the resistance 'rat line' or a special forces operative working with the Maquis post D-Day. I was determined to find out who this gentleman was and perhaps write about him for the history society which I was involved with at that time.

Little did I know that this seemingly simple quest would take me five years to complete and take me all over Europe meeting historians, writers, involve communications with people as far afield as America and Canada, luncheons in exclusive clubs and the undoubted honour of meeting former agents, their families and Maquis members.

As a former professional investigator, having experience of a range of crimes from a dog bite to multiple murders, I can say that there are many similarities between a major criminal investigation and historical research; the main one being they are both a search for the truth. The main differences are that in the former there is usually a suspect still living and the answers to questions are all there if you look hard enough. In the latter the answers can be lost and never retrievable and to accept this and move on to the next question is a skill I have learnt. I rank the search for who Desmond Ellis Hubble was as one of my fondest experiences and I do hope that the finished product is as enjoyable to read as it has been an honour to investigate.

Mick Manise

ACKNOWLEDGEMENTS

I once read an acknowledgements page which started by paying homage to the author's wife, I thought it odd at the time but I now understand where this person was speaking from. My wife Christine has spent years listening to my excitement about finding out yet another unknown fact about Desmond Hubble and spent many patient hours listening to me ranting at the inability of my computer to write a book for me; I owe her for her patience, advice and research guidance.

Without the support and patience of Desmond's family, in particular his daughter Jacquie, I would not have got very far and am very grateful for their support and encouragement and truly hope that this work is a tribute to the sacrifice made by Desmond and his family.

During the course of my research I have been very lucky with source contacts in particular my very good friend Philippe LeClerc, a French historian specialising in the resistance movements of the Ardennes during World War Two. Philippe has also been a great help in finding my French roots and understanding my heritage. I am also very grateful to Mr Mark Seaman the author of 'The Bravest of the Brave' for his permission to quote from his previous works and information regarding George Whitehead. Without Mr Seaman's permission and his ongoing kind encouragement I would have no information about George and little usable information about Desmond's subsequent journey into captivity and beyond.

I am also grateful to Mrs Beverley Matthews, MCLIP the senior librarian at Tonbridge School, for her dedicated searches of school records for clues. Mr Jerry Owen,

Languages master at The King's School Worcester for his translations.

Mr Luke Wall-Row for information regarding his father. Mr Duncan Stewart for advice regarding SOE, Citronelle and West Africa. Mr Doug Poulter for the initial connection to Desmond's family. M. Frédéric Docq for advice regarding French resistance. Ann Brudenell for her artistic map of the Ardennes. Rebecca Welch Ohio University Press for advice re source material and Nancy Ellen Lawler for her book 'Soldiers, Airmen, Spies and Whisperers' without which there is very little source material about West Africa during World War Two. Last but by no means least, Miss Suzanne Oatley for proof reading.

FOREWORD

In January 2010 I received an email from a distant cousin living in America to say he had received an enquiry from a retired British detective living in Portugal who was interested in finding out more about my father's life and death in order that he could write a book about a brave man of whom I knew little. It was with considerable curiosity that I contacted Mick Manise and then began an extraordinary association with a quite remarkable man with whom in the past four years, we have exchanged numerous emails, enjoyed memorable lunches and which has resulted in my family and I now having an extraordinary account of my father's life, his career in MI6 and SOE and importantly his death in Buchenwald.

In addition to our good fortune in knowing Mick, his investigations have resulted in my family and I meeting many of the men and women who shared my father's life both in France and Britain, thereby giving me a much better understanding of who my father was.

True to his police background, Mick has undertaken the most thorough research into my father's life, his school days, his life in Africa and France reading through innumerable documents, visiting the sites of my father's SOE exploits in the Ardennes. He has sought out former Resistant men and women who all remember my father and whom subsequently I have had the privilege of meeting.

Throughout his research Mick has always shown my family and I considerable sensitivity, kindness, thoughtfulness and always with a great sense of humour. In his first email to me Mick said

'I hope my intervention is a positive experience'. It most certainly has been and my family and I feel privileged that Mick has gone to so much trouble to produce such a comprehensive account of my father Desmond Hubble.

Jacquie Isaac nee Hubble
London 2014

CONTENTS

PART I

FAMILY AND EARLY LIFE

Desmond Ellis Hubble was born on Saturday 29th January 1910 at home. His parents were Reginald Hubble and Agnes Marie Hubble (nee Savell) of 61 Castelnau, Barnes, Middlesex. Reginald and Agnes were married on 8th July 1905 at Barley Parish Church, Hertfordshire. Reginald, who was 34 years old at the time, is described as a bachelor and a gentleman. His father was Stephen Isaac Hubble also with the title of gentleman. Agnes was 27 years old and described as a spinster, the daughter of Thomas Savell a farmer.

At this time in English history the title 'gentleman' was used to describe a man of status below nobility of wealth, often from property, but in all cases those of independent means without the need to work. In later years the title of gentleman has been widened to encompass any man of good manners and of course in plural for male convenience.

Reginald and Agnes had three children in total, Reginald Savell Hubble born in 1907, Desmond in 1910 and Mary Agnes Hubble was born in 1912. Desmond's birth certificate shows that his father's occupation was now an electrical engineer. He was baptised into the Church of England on 9th April 1910 at St Mary's Church, Barnes. On the 2nd of April 1922 he was confirmed at the same church but took his first communion on 9th April 1922 at Holy Trinity Church, Castelnau.

A very young Desmond (Photo Mrs Jacquie Isaac nee Hubble)

The first known school that Desmond attended was Colet Court, located in the south west of London. This is the preparatory school for St Paul's private school, London. Colet Court admits boys from the age of seven years and records show that Desmond left in 1923 to attend Tonbridge School as a boarder. It was at Colet Court that Desmond commenced his education in the French Language, his teacher being Paul Serrafique Manise, my Great Grandfather. This gentleman originated from a town in the Ardennes area of North Western France called Fumay, where he was a lawyer. In 1896 Paul came to England and settled in London, where he obtained the post of French Master at Colet Court. He married and his son, my grandfather, also attended Colet Court at the same time as Desmond. This coincidence becomes all the more remarkable later in Desmond's story. One other pupil who Paul Manise taught to speak French was Bernard Law Montgomery who attended St Paul's School. One other twist in Desmond's story worth mentioning here is that one of Desmond's grandsons, Alexander, became a master at Colet Court.

COLET COURT

Colet Court preparatory school for boys was founded in 1881 by an assistant master of St Paul's School, Samuel Bewsher, who was also the high master's secretary. The school was initially known as Colet House until 1891 and changed location a number of times as it expanded from its six initial pupils to 300. It has provided an excellent foundation and preparation for boys who go on to St Paul's or other prestigious private schools.

TONBRIDGE SCHOOL

In 1923 Desmond did not elevate to St Paul's but was sent as a boarder to Tonbridge. He was assigned to Park House and was enrolled into the Officer Training Corps (O.T.C.) as a private.

The OTC was an established means of introducing public school boys to military training and life. The formation of this branch of the British army was first suggested in 1907 by a committee set up by the then Secretary of State for War, Richard Haldene, to make up for a critical shortage of officers in both the regular and reserve forces. It was established by Royal Warrant in April 1908 and formed with a senior section for universities and a junior section for public schools. Until the Great War of 1914-18 membership of the OTC was a voluntary matter. The huge loss of life experienced during this conflict created an even greater shortage of men suitable for officer training and in order to resolve this situation membership of the OTC became a compulsory matter with few exceptions.

The OTC offered boys and young men an insight into military life by introducing them to military uniform with a discipline and structure similar to actual military life. At Tonbridge the OTC was organised into sections, platoons and companies. Each Section had Corporals, every two sections had a Sergeant and there were four sections in each platoon. The number of platoons in a company varied but in charge of each company were a Company Sergeant Major and two Under Officers. All of these ranks were students of the school. Each OTC had a commanding officer with an adjutant second in command and company officers, usually retired professional soldiers. Warrant Officers acted in specialist roles as drill instructors, parade duties, physical training and band. The OTC was regarded by those who later went into the army as a good basic training for life in the forces and taught such skills as drill, field craft and weapon training.

By 1927 Desmond had achieved an OTC certificate A with 371 marks out of a possible 600 and been promoted to Corporal in charge of section 3, number 8 platoon of C Company. He was in science set mid 5 under Mr A. Beresford Ryley M.A. and maths set B2 under Rev F.N. Berry M.A.

He was a keen pianist and played Rachmaninov's Prelude in G minor in the house music competition of March 1927 receiving marks of 36/50.

He became a house præposter of Park House under the House Master Mr H.R. Stokoe M.A. and at this time there were 47 boys in Park house and six præposters (term used in schools teaching Latin and meaning 'placed before', but here, a prefect). Above this achievement were school præposter and of course a head boy.

His school achievements have shown that he was a capable and intelligent boy but not destined to be an academic star.

Desmond at Tonbridge (Photo Mrs J. Isaac)

WORKING LIFE

Desmond left Tonbridge in summer 1927 from the Science Middle Fifth, which suggests that he was in the middle stream of academic ability. Those who left without reaching the Sixth Form would not have been thought of as university material in those days. On leaving Tonbridge Desmond went to work for the family business of Messrs. Hall and Harding as an under-manager.

Hall and Harding was a subsidiary company of B.J. Hall and Co. of Stourton House, Dacre St., Victoria Street, London, SW1 which was formed by Benjamin James Hall. Hall was the husband of Desmond's aunt Annie Hall nee Hubble. The company was involved in the manufacture and distribution of mathematical measuring equipment.

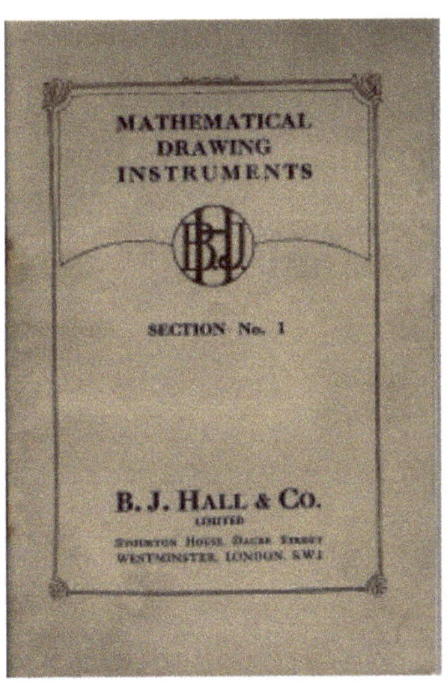

Sales Brochure for B.J. Hall & Co.
(Picture courtesy of David Riches)

Available records show that Desmond was variously employed in the capacities of accountant, company secretary, photo-printer's representative and director of B.J. Hall & Co. He also later declared directorships of:

- Thames Valley Development Co. Ltd.
- Drawing Office Supplies Ltd.
- D.O.S. Associates Ltd.

On a subsequent military application form he declares a "*Thorough knowledge of all departments of the photo printing and drawing office manufacturing trade*". This implies that during the 12 years from leaving school until joining the army at the outbreak of war, he served a tailor-made apprenticeship with the family companies and developed a good head for business. It was during this period that Desmond developed a good knowledge of photography and became a keen amateur photographer. Despite his background, Desmond later declared his political views as 'Labour'.

A young Desmond on the beach (Photo Mrs J. Isaac)

MARRIAGE

On 27th June 1931 aged 21, Desmond was married to Margaret Elsie Seiflow who was 24 years old at the Parish Church, Pinner,

Middlesex. At this time Reginald Hubble is shown as a company's director as was the bride's father, Max Seiflow. Max Seiflow was a German immigrant living with his family in the Hatch End area near to Pinner. He was a businessman who had been instrumental in the rescue of a company run by a German wine grower named Julius Kayser. The company had bases in both London and in Traben-Trarbach in the Moselle area of Germany. This company fell into bankruptcy in 1931 and re-emerged as M&H Seiflow. The relevance of this is apparent later in the story.

The Seiflow family, Desmond far right Margaret far left front row. Max Seiflow elderly gentleman centre with hand on his wife's shoulder. (Courtesy Hubble family).

CHILDREN

On 21st February 1933 Desmond's first child was born, Michael Desmond, at 13 Roxborough Park, Harrow. At this stage the family were living at 5, Wellington Court, Hatch End, Middlesex. Desmond is shown as a Company Secretary.

On 31st December 1934 the second child, Peter Reginald, was born at the same address as Michael. Desmond is now a photo printer's representative and the family address is Green Woods, Pinner Green, Pinner.

The couple's third child, Jacqueline Margaret, was born on 24th January 1940 at 54, Marsh Road, Pinner, Harrow and the family's address was Highfield, The Avenue, Hatch End. Desmond is by now a company's director and a Second Lieutenant in the 75th Middlesex Regiment, Royal Artillery.

During the 1930s Desmond travelled to a variety of countries for holidays. In France the Brittany Coast, Marne and Loire Valley. In Germany the Moselle Valley and Traben Trarbach and in Switzerland Grundelwald, Thun and Interlaken districts. He also recorded that he travelled to Belgium on business where no doubt his French would have been very useful. He had developed a fluency in French when speaking and reading plus a working knowledge for writing. His German was described as a working knowledge when both spoken and read.

He had developed a number of interests and skills at various stages of his life to-date:

Wine festival in Traben Trarbach 1937 (photo Mrs J. Isaac)

- Wine tasting
- Photography, both professional and recreational
- Mountaineering
- Running
- Boxing
- Swimming
- Piano playing
- Cycling
- Playing Chess

Wine tasting was the purpose of a three week holiday spent in the Moselle area at Traben-Trarbach in 1937 where he stayed with family on Margaret's side, the Seiflows.

Mountaineering was a pastime pursued on a two month holiday in Switzerland and the family albums contain a very nice picture of Desmond and his mother sitting outside a mountain chalet wearing sturdy walking boots. This picture shows that he maintained a good level of fitness and not allowed the good life and social duties of business life to spoil his physique.

Running, boxing and swimming were skills developed at Tonbridge.

One of Desmond's treasured possessions was a travelling chess set which his mother had given him and was later to be a valued asset and lifeline to sanity for him and others.

PART II

WAR

POLITICAL SITUATION

The situation throughout Europe during the 1920s and 30s was very much a product of the result of the First World War. During 1918 the German forces had progressed a final massive push forward, which had left many soldiers with the impression that finally a breakthrough was imminent and victory for Germany within their grasp. The sudden request for an armistice was a mystery for many soldiers who considered that they had been let down. A certain Corporal and holder of the Iron Cross, Adolf Hitler, used the betrayal to fuel his insane hatred of Communists and Jews and formed an opinion that the German people had been 'stabbed in the back' by the instigators of an international conspiracy of Communist Jews. At the time of hearing the news of Germany's capitulation, Hitler was recovering in hospital from a gas attack; he did not return to the front but came back to Germany a bitter and hate filled man.

The subsequent Treaty of Versailles, which determined how Germany would make reparation for starting the war, treated the country in a solely punitive manner with no attempt at reconciliation or rehabilitation. Germany struggled to pay the reparations and its economy spiralled into crippling inflation; a loaf of bread cost millions of Deutschmarks. Soldiers returning from the front retained their weapons and became armed gangs affiliated to various political causes, unemployment was very high and the savings of the middle classes became worthless. On returning to Germany Hitler became a spy reporting on the activities of various political groups. It was one of these groups, the Deutsche Arbeitrpartei or German Workers Party (DAP), which caught his attention and he subsequently joined. With the aid of a paramilitary organisation the Sturmabteilung (SA) under the leadership of Ernst Röhm, Hitler manipulated himself to the leadership of the DAP and changed the party's name to the Nationalsozialistische Deutsche Arbeiterpartei or NSDAP more commonly known as the Nazi party.

As dissent in Germany grew so did the extremes of political support. The German Communist party became the idealogical opposite of the Nazi party and thereby their hated enemy. Street and bar brawls became not only common but the order of the day. German politics became confused and election after election was forced by disagreement by the opposing factions in the Reichstag. The Nazis became influentially sufficient in the parliament to keep forcing new general elections by walking out enmasse of the debating chamber, they made full use of the difficiencies of the democratic process to further their aims for power. Eventually the President, Paul Von Hindenburg, was reluctantly pursuaded to offer Hitler the Chancellorship, which had always been Hitler's aim. The reasoning behind this offer was that those in power thought they could control Hitler from this position and he would fail and fall by the wayside. This proved wrong and when in August 1934 Hindenburg died, Hitler abolished the post of President and appointed himself sole leader of Germany or, as he chose, the Führer.

Hitler and the Nazis then started to create a dictatorial state, passing laws to make their hold on power absolute and to marginalise the established democratic state and Hitler's political opponents. Herman Goering, as a government minister in the Nazi party, rolled out a programme of anti-Semitic laws denying German Jews basic human rights and freedoms. Jews in professions such as education, policing and the military were dismissed; they were barred from the legal profession and Jewish doctors were banned from treating Aryan Germans. Inter-race relationships were banned and marriage to a Jew was illegal. Jews were defined by heritage; a person with two Jewish parents was a Jew, and a person with one Jewish parent was a half Jew and so on. To be classed as German there had to be no trace of Jewish ancestry for at least two generations. The world started to worry about Germany and those with foresight predicted that war was inevitable; German Jews started to leave Germany and were forced to purchase visas at extortionate prices.

In 1936 Hitler's army re-occupied the Rhineland which had been de-militarised by the Treaty of Versailles and on 12th March 1938 Hitler entered Austria, near to his birth place at Braunau and the Anschluss is completed. Six months later Hitler, with the support of his ally, Italy's Dictator Benito Mussolini, entered into negotiations with the Prime Ministers of France and Britain, who, in a disgraceful act of appeasement, on 30th September 1938 signed the Munich agreement allowing Hitler to expand his borders into the Sudetenland. Within days German troops marched into Czechoslovakia and commenced an occupation which left the rest of the country open to invasion.

Not everyone in Britain was in agreement with the complacency of appeasement which was reflected in November 1938 when the safe Conservative seat of West Somerset (held in the general election of 1935 with a 10,000 majority) was successfully contested by Mr Vernon Bartlett, who described his political views as Independent Progressive. Bartlett was elected by 19,540 voters who shared his policy of opposition to the government's soft line towards German aggression. This was sufficiently newsworthy to make the German press and it is recorded that Hitler, on hearing the news, scowled!

An article printed in one London newspaper on February 2nd 1939 entitled 'Reviews of the Month' referred to the review of January and was dominated by opinions of the current political situation following the Munich agreement. Desmond is quoted as making a strong plea for a road system, far in advance of what existed at the time, in view of social industrial and strategic needs. He was clearly a man of vision and having seen first-hand the situation in Germany, including its new road system, designed not only to create jobs but to put in place an effective transport network for the rapid deployment of troops. He knew that Hitler was not going to settle for the territories he had gained with the acceptance of the great powers and that war was inevitable and Britain was in great peril.

WORLD WAR TWO

On 1st September 1939 Germany invaded Poland using as an excuse a faked attack on a German radio station. Prisoners were dressed in Polish army uniforms and shot at the site of the alleged attack. Britain and France both being allied to Poland gave Germany an ultimatum to withdraw its forces under penalty of war. Germany failed to comply and on 3rd September 1939 Britain and France declared war on Germany.

On 2nd September 1939 Desmond enlisted in the Royal Artillery and became Gunner Hubble. His regiment was a Territorial unit, the 75th Middlesex Search Light Regiment and he was assigned to 470 Battery based at Cowley. His attestation number which became his army service number was 1519723. His address on enlistment was Holywell, Uxbridge Road, Hatch End, Barnes, London.

ROYAL ARTILLERY REGIMENT

The title Royal Artillery was bestowed in 1720 to units of field artillery which had been raised at Woolwich by the Royal Warrant of King George I on 26th May 1716. At this time two regular companies, each 100 men strong, were formed. Prior to this date artillery units were raised by Royal Warrant for specific campaigns, the first recorded use being at the Battle of Crecy in 1346 during the 100 Years' War.

In 1939 radar was a very new innovation and search lights were being directed by either heat seeking or sound detecting devices. Eventually these locating methods were replaced with radar.

British soldiers directing a searchlight (photo internet)

The objectives of the search light crews were to light up any aircraft in order that they could be attacked by night fighters or ground anti-aircraft guns and to dazzle the pilots in order to disorientate them away from their targets. They also sent Morse signals via the lamp to guide friendly aircraft home; each area was given a different location code to enable coordination of effort. The lamps were also used horizontally to light up damaged areas to assist the location of trapped people. This was a very hazardous duty for the searchers as direct eye contact with the lamp could result in blindness. Two types of search light were in use, 90cm and 150cm and they were powered by a large generator. The crews for these lights were up to 14 persons individually numbered according to role, numbers one to nine being essential personnel. Crew members one, two and three were the NCOs Lance Corporal, Corporal and Sergeant acting as spotters. Four operated the elevating arm; five received information from the listening crews and relayed it to four using radio sets. Six, seven and eight were the listening or radar crew who sat in a tent at the rear. Number nine was the generator operator.

On 8th September 1939 Desmond was promoted to Bombardier (Corporal) and on 21st November 1939 he was promoted again to Lance Sergeant.

In December 1939 under Kings Regulation 383 with a total service of 112 days Desmond was discharged from the army and granted an emergency commission in the rank of 2nd Lieutenant with 470 Battery Royal Artillery. His address was now given on promotion as 'Highfield', The Avenue, Hatch End.

Newly promoted 2nd Lieutenant 1519723
Hubble R.A. (Photo Mrs J. Isaac)

There is no obvious connection between the Royal Artillery Regiment and Desmond; however I suspect this was his choice. As a volunteer he was able to make requests of personal preferences for posting. He was stationed at Cowley, not far from home and on commission he declared the directorships he held and signed a document by which he declared that his directorships would not influence his position as a commissioned officer. This effectively meant that he was able to serve and not be that far away and he could still have an influence on company business.

The war had been predicted for some time at this stage and it was rightly expected that aerial bombardment would be a major factor that Britain would have to defend against. The art of aerial bombing had started in the First World War and bombs actually dropped on Britain by Zeppelin balloons. The Germans had secretly developed a Luftwaffe, contrary to the terms of the Treaty of Versailles, under the guise of civil aviation and had despatched its Condor Legions to assist General Franco in the Spanish Civil War. Here the art of aerial bombardment had been developed against civilian populations. Early in 1939 an advisory document had been circulated to the public at the same time as gas masks had been issued to every man, woman and child, informing the public that there was no defence against gas for pets and that it would be far kinder to have them put down in advance of hostilities. The result of this was a huge increase in the mouse and rat populations of London and the price of a kitten on the black market was exorbitant! It gives a feel for the fear of gas which had been used by both sides during the First War and the expectation of bombing as a tactic.

On 16th February 1940 Desmond submitted a declaration form giving details of his business interests and directorships held. On 1st May 1940 Desmond attended a Cipher training course at the Household Cavalry barracks in Hyde Park, London and after successful completion of the course on 10th May he was posted as cipher officer to number 2 Swayne Military Mission. At dawn that day German forces invaded the Netherlands, Belgium, Luxembourg and France by land and air and Winston Churchill was appointed Prime Minister to head a coalition government.

SWAYNE AND FRANCE

The Swayne Military Mission was headed by Brigadier John George des Reaux Swayne and its purpose was to create a liaison staff for the BEF at the French military headquarters of General Georges, the Commander of Land Forces North East under the overall command of General Gamelin. Second Lieutenant Hubble's duties were the ciphering and deciphering of messages in and out of the mission's headquarters.

The static trench warfare of World War One was created by the invention and use of the machine gun. Both sides possessed this weapon in both quantity and quality and once the initial German thrust was halted, the front lines did not advance or retreat much throughout the war because the advantage over advancing infantry was created by strategically placed machine guns, with sufficient fields of fire to ensure that any advance had to walk through a wall of lead. Armoured and aerial warfare was not developed effectively until the end of the war and then it was in its infancy from a tactical and engineering point. Following the end of this conflict, France decided to defend itself with a gigantic wall, named the Maginot Wall after the French Minister implementing the initiative. The wall started at the border with Switzerland and it was intended for it to finish at the French coast. Finance prevented the completion of this wall and it actually ended at the Ardennes region of France and Belgium. The Ardennes is a very mountainous, forested and rugged area with small roads or tracks where roads did not exist, it was thought impossible for a modern mechanised army to penetrate this region and the German attack was expected through central Belgium as it had occurred in the first war. The other weakness of the Maginot line was that the guns of the fortifications had a fixed line of fire into Germany, the expected aggressor, and could not be turned to defend an attack from the rear.

The Blitz Krieg tactic was successful for the Germans and they took full advantage of the mobility of armour supported by aerial bombardment. Light bombers, particularly the Stuka dive bomber, strafed and bombed ahead of advancing forces creating panic and retreat of both military personnel and civilians. Retreating columns of civilians were machine gunned by these aviators; a tactic designed to keep roads clear in order not to slow the advance. The German advance was rapid and in a matter of weeks they had reached the coast splitting France in two. The BEF was trapped on the northern coast and on 27th May the evacuation of British and French forces was conducted from the beaches at Dunkirk ending on 4th June. This was codenamed Operation Dynamo and with the help of a fleet of small boats and volunteers the Royal Navy brought 338,226 British and French soldiers to England.

On 10thJune 1940 Italy entered the war on the side of Germany and declared war on Britain and France. Following a successful German thrust in the Somme area the French Government evacuated to Bordeaux declaring Paris an open city thereby saving it from destruction. Desmond and the rest of the Swayne mission remained with the retreating French Headquarters staff also in Bordeaux. It was looking very much like a POW camp was his immediate future.

EVACUATION

A second evacuation plan, Operation Ariel, was developed on the north and west coast of France and between 14th to 25th June 215,000 British and Canadian troops were removed to the safety of Britain from Cherbourg, St Malo, St Nazaire, Brest and Nantes. Desmond was evacuated by ship from St Nazaire after 17th June. As Operation Ariel commenced on 14th June the German Wermacht entered an undefended Paris. All the time Desmond was retreating and waiting for evacuation, he was subjected to constant aerial bombardment by the Luftwaffe. While he waited for a place on a ship at St Nazaire the former Cunard luxury liner, RMS Lancastria, was bombed by Junkers JU 88 bombers. The Lancastria, like many other merchant ships, had been requisitioned as a troop carrier at the beginning of the war and was on this occasion being loaded with civilian refugees, troops and RAF personnel. It is estimated that at the time of this attack the ship which was designed for 2,200 people including crew had between 4,000 and 9,000 souls on board, such was the chaotic situation which prevailed. She was hit by three bombs at 3.48 p.m. and listed first to starboard and then to port which created an uncontrollable roll, the ship capsized and sank inside 20 minutes and there were only 2,477 survivors. This tragedy has been recorded as the largest loss of life due to the sinking of a British ship and reporting was initially suppressed by a D notice. It was terrifying for Desmond and his colleagues to witness this event and then take their own chances when they boarded a ship for home and safety.

On 16thJune Churchill visited the French Commanders and government at Bordeaux, in an effort to encourage France to continue the fight. The situation by now was deemed hopeless and Churchill's efforts were not successful. French Prime Minister Paul Reynaud resigned, refusing to accept that the war was lost. He was superseded by Marshall Philippe Pétain who on 17th June notified the French people over the radio of his intention to sue for an armistice. Another emerging French patriot was also refusing to accept defeat on that day in Bordeaux, Général Charles-André-Joseph-Marie de Gaulle, the only French commander to force a retreat of German forces during the battle for France. He defied the Pétain order to remain in France and boarded a plane bound for London with 100,000 gold Francs given to him by Reynaud to continue the fight from England. For this defiance de Gaulle was prosecuted in absentia and sentenced initially to four years in prison and at a second hearing to death for treason, but from London he formed the Free French Forces.

On 18th June Churchill told the House of Commons, "*The battle for France is over, I expect that the Battle for Britain is about to begin*". On the same day General de Gaulle made a speech to the French people via the BBC.

Not many French people heard the speech on the day as many were refugees and the BBC was not widely listened to in France, at this stage. His words were repeated over the next few days and it was also placed in French newspapers in the as yet unoccupied South. It has become the most famous of speeches in

French history and gave hope to those determined to see a Free France again.

When Hitler heard of the French request for an armistice he chose the forest at Compiègne as the location to sign the surrender. He had the same railway carriage used for the 1918 humiliation of Germany taken from a museum to the very same spot where Germany had been forced to sign the 1918 armistice. This Armistice was signed on 22nd June and came into force on 25th June; the carriage was then blown up.

It is often said that Britain now stood alone but the British Empire and Commonwealth stretched around the globe and totalled nearly 500 million people. At this time there was also a real threat to peace in the Far East. Japan, in its attempts to create its own Empire in the east had invaded and occupied China during the 1930s. Following the fall of France the Vichy government allowed Japan to enter and occupy French Indo-China and in the same month, September 1940, Japan allied itself with Nazi Germany. Japan's policy of expansionism was clearly a threat to the British Empire in the east and the importance of Africa for raw materials, such as rubber, was even more prominent. Japan did not become an active belligerent until its attacks on the US fleet at Pearl Harbour and British colonies on 7th September 1941 but in the meantime the political situation between the two sides was strained, with war an anticipated eventuality.

Initially, following the fall of France, Hitler did not do anything, he clearly was expecting Britain to surrender or sue for peace; there was no pre prepared plan for an invasion of Britain. A month after the fall of France, Britain having failed to surrender, Hitler developed his plan for invasion and the Battle of Britain, codenamed Operation Sea Lion, commenced on 13th August.

Operation Sea Lion was dependent on three factors, superiority in the air and at sea plus weather. Hitler issued a four point directive:

1. The RAF was to be destroyed or reduced to an ineffective force.
2. The Royal Navy to be engaged in the North Sea and Atlantic.

3. Coastal areas of England to be dominated by heavy artillery.
4. The English Channel to be swept of British mines and blockaded at both ends by German mines.

The battle opened with aerial attacks on RAF bases with a view to destroying the fighting capacity of British air power both on the ground and in the air.

This picture of the situation at home gives an idea of the value which Desmond's skills were seen. He was a trained officer in a search light regiment and these were to become an important front line link in the defence of Britain. At a time when the defence of Britain was taking priority for manpower and resources, Desmond was selected for duties in Africa with the McKenzie Mission. It also gives an indication of the value which Britain placed on Africa as a source of war materials, food and friends. The expectation of an attack on British Colonies on the West Coast from French Vichy forces was planned for and expected from 1940 until the Axis threat was eliminated from the continent.

PART III

AFRICA

Desmond arrived in England around 20th June 1940 and on 29th June he was promoted to Lieutenant and posted to the No 19 (McKenzie) Military Mission in the Belgian Congo as cipher officer. He embarked from Southampton on the SS Durban Castle bound for South Africa on 4th July 1940. The convoy was escorted by Royal Naval ships of the home fleet stationed at Scapa Flow and stopped at Takoradi in the British Colony of Gold Coast where the escort vessels were changed to those of the South Atlantic Fleet stationed at Cape Town. Takoradi has an important deep water harbour and during World War Two had an airfield from which the South African air force flew anti-submarine and convoy escort duties.

JOURNEY BY CONVOY

The Durban Castle was a luxury liner built in Belfast in 1938 for Union Castle and used on the South Africa mail run. The trip around Africa lasted over three weeks and under normal circumstances a best suite with bathroom and toilet cost £100. I doubt whether the Army would have paid for a mere Lieutenant to travel in such style.

At the outbreak of war nearly all merchant vessels travelled, at first, voluntarily and later by compulsion, in convoy. The

Pictures courtesy of Björn Larsson (timetableimages.com)

ABOVE: *Two-berth Cabin, "Durban Castle"*

convoys were initially unarmed and involved between 30 and 70 ships. The main danger from enemy attack was in the mid to north Atlantic sea routes, but the danger of attack extended down the west coast of Africa from the mouth of the Mediterranean. Limited support could be given to ships by land based aircraft from the coasts of America, Britain, Gibraltar, and West coast African colonies such as Sierra Leone and Gold Coast.

The dangers for Desmond's sea journey came from new German sea ports being developed in the Biscay area of France and of course the issue with the French Navy had not at this stage been resolved. The French fleet had been requested to sail for a British port and become a part of the Free French forces but had refused. Most of the French fleet sailed for Vichy controlled ports in North and West Africa. The largest allied worry was that they would fall into the hands of German or Italian forces. This problem was resolved on 3rd July 1940 when the Royal Navy attacked and sank most of the French Fleet moored at Mers-el-Kébir killing 1,297 and wounding 350 French mariners.

The perceived threats can be ascertained from War Cabinet minutes of July 1940. U-boats were active as were motor torpedo boats (MTB's). These vessels had a shallow draft and mine fields were not a problem for them at low tides. Germany possessed approximately 100 MTB's and America had just withdrawn a promise of 20 such boats for Britain which were to be used to counter the threat in home waters. German pocket battle ships such as Tirpitz were not believed to be at sea. Aerial bombing attacks from land based aircraft were a threat in certain coastal areas whilst in the Mediterranean the Italian fleet had not, at this stage, been neutralised and the Italian Air Force was seen as a skilful, determined and well-resourced threat.

A very real threat was faced by the convoy whilst in British waters. The start date of the Battle of Britain was initially recorded by Air Chief Marshal Sir Hugh Dowding as the 8th August 1940; he later changed his mind and declared the date as 10th July, six days after Desmond sailed. Prior to this date the Luftwaffe were patrolling the coast of England in search of shipping targets and developing intelligence on the routes of shipping and the best places to make attacks. On 20th March in the late evening the SS Barn Hill was attacked, bombed and sunk by a Heinkel He 111H bomber three miles from Beachy Head. Total shipping losses for the month of June 1940 in the Atlantic were 53 British, Allied and neutral ships totalling 297,000 tons from all causes; three armed merchant cruisers, against the loss of two German U-boats.

AFRICA WORLD WAR TWO

The situation in Africa before the Second World War was also affected by the conclusion of World War One. Africa was run by colonial powers and Germany had been stripped of its colonies by the Treaty of Versailles. The two former German Colonies in West Africa, Cameroon and Togoland were under the Jurisdiction of France and Great Britain. The other element of the Treaty of Versailles having a bearing was that Italy, as a member of the allies of World War One, felt insufficiently rewarded by the treaty and that it should have been given more colonial power. In 1935 Italy invaded Ethiopia to add to its colony of Libya and on 10th June 1940 Italy declared war on Britain and France, despite offers of greater colonial influence in Africa in exchange for their neutrality. Benito Mussolini, the Italian Dictator, had withheld formal alliance from one side or the other and was probably swayed to the Axis side by Hitler's initial successes and his entry to Paris. He had visions of a new Italian Empire on the lines of ancient Rome and did not wish to be left out of the equation when Europe was carved up by the winners. On 9th June Italian forces in Libya commenced attacks on the British in Egypt, the Italian forces were quickly repulsed. This demonstrated Mussolini's desire for greater colonial power in Africa and his ultimate ambition to take Egypt and the Suez Canal.

In West Africa the colonial powers were Great Britain, France, Belgium, Portugal and Spain. Britain's four colonies, Gold Coast, Sierra Leone, Gambia and Nigeria, were surrounded by French territories and as no one had foreseen the fall of France and that country becoming a belligerent power, there was almost no British intelligence service in this part of Africa.

Portugal and Spain were neutral countries in this conflict although both were run by right wing dictators. In Spain's case, General Franco had conducted a civil war in Spain between July 1937 and April 1939 leading the nationalist army against the established republican regime. During the course of this conflict Franco had accepted assistance from Hitler, but fell short of giving Germany direct support and joining the Axis, Franco was certainly pro Fascism. The British used this knowledge to great effect when wishing to spread disinformation to the Germans. A typical example is the story of 'the man who never was'. This relates to Operation Mincemeat where the body of a vagrant Glyndwr Michael, was dressed in the uniform of a Royal Commando major and given the fictitious identity of "Major Martin". Major Martin acted as a courier of documents which indicated an invasion of Greece when the real target was Sicily. The Germans were fed the information secretly via Spanish authorities, who found the body washed up on a beach. The Germans were totally taken in resulting in the movement of forces to defend the wrong place.

Portugal was run by a right wing dictator, Dr. Salazar. Salazar was a university professor and economist recruited to government by a desperate parliament and who served as Prime Minister from 1932 to 1968. He turned Portugal's failing economy around in a very short period of time by ruling with an iron fist. He developed an effective secret police and liberal use of concentration camps for political opponents. Whilst he maintained strict neutrality, his politics leant towards the right, repressing communism, socialism, anarchism and liberalism. Portugal was a rich source of minerals, including Wolfram which was used to make armour plate for tanks. Following Germany's invasion of Russia, which had formerly supplied Germany's needs, Portugal exported this ore to them. However to maintain neutrality the allies were supplied in equal quantities; in fact in 1943 when Salazar was persuaded by the allies that Germany was going to lose the war and that it would be in Portugal's best interests to cease supplying Germany, he did cease to supply but also stopped supplying the allies as well.

BELGIAN CONGO

Belgium was a relatively new country being formed in 1830 with the strict proviso that it remained a neutral state, this at a time when the big European powers were expanding their colonial empires, including Africa. Large scale colonialism would have affected this neutral status and as the Belgian economy was reliant on trade with its neighbours, any falling out with trade partners would have had a disastrous effect. Enterprising Belgian businessmen formed trading posts around the world in order to compete on the international markets, but various attempts to form colonies failed, often ending in disaster for the adventurers concerned. Belgium also lacked the logistical ability to form colonies, funding would not come from the mother country which also lacked the military power to start and then keep their interests secure. In 1862 Belgium dismantled its small naval fleet and as its commercial fleet was very small, reliance was placed on other countries' shipping to support their international interests. In 1865 King Leopold II ascended to the throne, he had been a keen traveller and saw forced labour and colonialism as a means to benefit his country. During the 1870s the main European powers of Central Africa, Britain, France, Germany and Portugal allowed King Leopold to form the Congo Free State in the huge area which became the Belgian Congo in 1908 and then ultimately the Republic of Congo in 1960 on gaining its independence. Leopold's methods were nefarious to say the least and later the ruling of the country became brutal in order to achieve commercial success. The practice of cutting off the hands of villagers who did not produce sufficient rubber was common and there is even evidence of mass murder on a holocaust scale.

The Belgian Congo (Picture courtesy of Prober Encyclopaedia)

The Congo straddles the equator and covers nearly 1,000,000 square kilometres in Central Africa with a narrow strip of land along the Congo River giving the only access to sea on the west coast. It has a vast plateau in its centre covered by rainforest and the rest of the country is made up of mountain ranges, savannas, plains and grass lands. Due largely to the diversity of terrain and climate the wildlife is reflective of that diversity and to a keen photographer such as Desmond it must have been a wonderland of opportunity. He certainly took a camera as family members remember seeing albums depicting life in Africa.

After World War One, European and American businesses invested in the Congo. Large plantations growing livestock, cotton, palm oil, coffee cocoa and rubber were developed. Mining industries were created for gold, silver, diamonds (mainly industrial), copper, tin, cobalt and zinc, iron ore, cadmium, and manganese. Another mining product was uranium and at the outbreak of World War Two an American businessman managed to take possession of a large stockpile and spirit it to the United States where he stored it in a New York warehouse. I often wonder if this is where the Manhattan Project derived its name! It is a fact, however, that Congo Uranium was used to develop the atomic bomb.

When Germany launched its attack on France via Belgium, the Belgian government escaped to Britain where they set up a government in exile. The collaborationist force in Belgium was called Rex and its members Rexists. The Congo remained loyal to the Government in Exile and its produce was made available to the allied cause by the administration there. This situation created an even greater exploitation of workers resulting in strikes and brutal suppression.

Desmond arrived in Cape Town on 16th July 1940 and remained in South Africa until 25th August 1940 also visiting Johannesburg. Whilst in South Africa he familiarised himself with operations there. Raw materials essential to Britain's war effort were gathered in South Africa prior to shipping back to England. During this time he became acquainted with Virginia McKenna who was nine years old. Miss McKenna lived with her father in London but at the outbreak of war was sent to live with her mother for the duration in Africa. They met at the home of the family who the McKenna's were staying with in Hout Bay, Cape Town. Desmond was introduced to the family by an unknown officer as shown in the photograph.

Desmond and a young Virginia McKenna
(Photo courtesy of Ms V. McKenna)

Ms McKenna subsequently became a famous film actress and starred as the SOE agent Violette Szabo in the film *Carve Her Name with Pride*. (This has a greater relevance further in Desmond's story).

Another location visited by Desmond whilst in South Africa was the Onderstepoort Veterinary Services near to Pretoria. Here he obtained a map of Africa and commenced to plot his travels throughout his stay on the continent. The map is still in the possession of family (Mr Julian Hubble, a grandson) and is too fragile to reproduce safely. Unfortunately there is no key but it is clear Desmond used a variety of line styles and colours to signify different modes of transport. For instance the first lines drawn on the map are straight red lines with directional arrows on the sea, this shows the direction and route of the ship including the stop at Jakoradi and the last leg to Cape Town.

On leaving South Africa Desmond travelled overland to take up his post as Cipher officer at the mission HQ in Leopoldville, Belgian Congo.

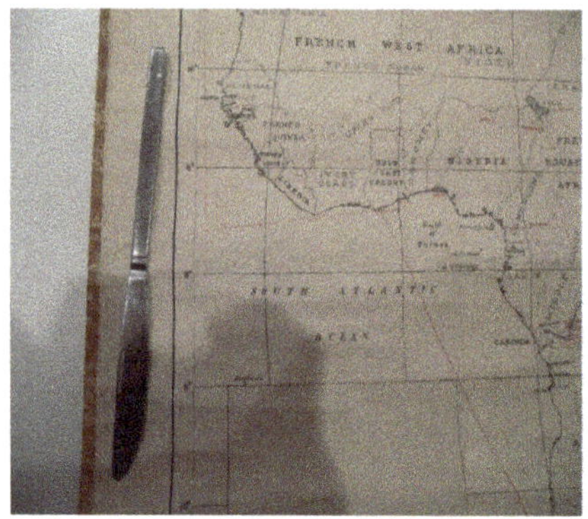 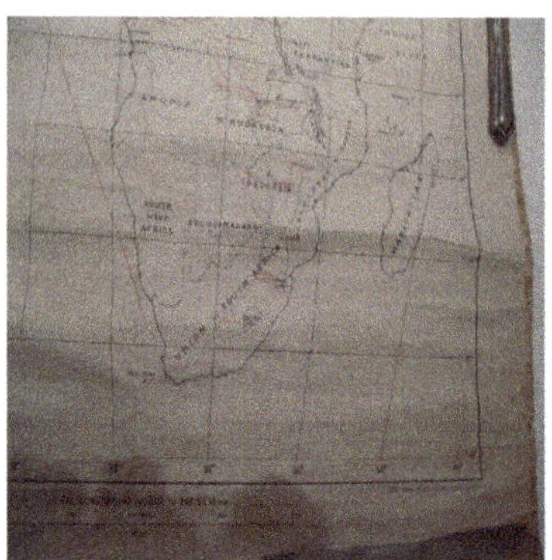

Desmond's map showing sea route to Cape Town & train journey to Pretoria. (Author photos)

In June 1941 the McKenzie mission was dissolved and Desmond was then transferred to the staff of GHQ West Africa no 19 British Liaison staff. He was promoted Captain to the role of GSO3 on 6th June 1941. His duties were very much of a liaison nature with the Belgian forces. On 15th November 1941 he attended a dinner in honour of King Leopold III with the 3rd Regiment of Leopoldville at the Grand Hotel in Leopoldville. The local news reported the visit of Lieutenant General Giffard, Commander in Chief of British troops in West Africa. The report mentions many very senior military and political figures, both British and Belgian and Capitaine Hubble who would have appeared to have co-ordinated the visit. He became very popular with Belgian officers and a letter was sent concerning him to GHQ by Major-General Gilliaert. This officer was the commander of the Belgian expeditionary force and had played a major role in preventing the retreat of Italian forces in Ethiopia, collecting 7,000 prisoners of war.

In total Desmond served 23 months in Africa and from his military record, letters and photographs, it is ascertainable that he also travelled to Angola travelling overland from Noqui to Luanda staying at both Luanda and Ambrizette. In Egypt he is pictured standing in front of the Sphinx and riding a camel near to the Pyramids. He also spent two weeks in Nigeria and the Gold Coast.

Photos courtesy of Mrs J. Isaac

On completion of his duties his commanding officer, Major W.R. Crocker submitted a very complimentary report about him, paragraphs 1 and 2 were a résumé of his work but paragraphs 3 and 4 give a good picture of the man.

> "3. *Captain Hubble combines personal address with good nature and good manners; his French is adequate; and he has a good head for business. He made himself popular with Belgians in all quarters. Major-General Gilliaert's letter, already sent to G.H.Q., indicates the terms on which he was with the Etat-Major.*
>
> 4. *Captain Hubble thus has a useful equipment for liaison and for other work. I believe, however, that this equipment would be made still more useful if he were attached to a formation for some months so that, after an absence of two years in a very special environment, he can get into the war atmosphere again and can get abreast of military matters.*
>
> *Leopoldville,*
> *Belgian Congo.*
> *2nd June 1942."*

He sailed from the Congo on 5th June 1942 arriving in England on the 17th June and commenced a period of leave.

15th July 1942 Desmond submitted a written request to engage in duties for W Section, Special Operations Executive, (SOE).

PART IV

SPECIAL OPERATIONS EXECUTIVE

Whilst the fall of France was a great shock, forward thinking had created an embryo for the formation of the SOE at a time when it was desperately needed. As early as March 1938 plans were being developed for the fighting of war in a non-conventional manner by the British. The use of propaganda and encouragement of unrest within both military and civilian populations and also the development of guerrilla warfare tactics as used by the IRA in Ireland, or indeed Lawrence of Arabia during World War One, was under consideration.

The simplistic explanation for the formation of SOE is Winston Churchill's famous order to form a new organisation to "set Europe ablaze". This, however, gives all the credit to Churchill and creates an injustice to the immense work by others who had the foresight to anticipate the need. The full story is complex, political and fully documented by renowned historians, it is sufficient for the purpose of Desmond's story to give a brief summary of the important events.

The fall of France had been foreseen by the military command from 25th May 1940 and that the encouragement of revolt inside occupied territories would become a strategic necessity for Britain's war effort. On 1st July 1940 a meeting to discuss this need was held at the Foreign Office under the chairmanship of

Lord Halifax, the Foreign Secretary. Amongst others three ministers were present including Dr Hugh Dalton the Minister for Economic Warfare. (The Foreign Office is responsible for external intelligence i.e. MI6 and the Home Office for internal Intelligence i.e. MI5). The following day Dr Dalton wrote to Lord Halifax and this letter was later used by those made responsible for the development of SOE as a format for their planning and gives a good picture of what was formed:

"We have got to organise movements in enemy occupied territory comparable to the Sinn Fein movement in Ireland, to the Chinese Guerrillas now operating against Japan, to the Spanish Irregulars who played a notable part in Wellington's campaign or one might as well admit it – to the organisations which the Nazis themselves have developed so remarkably in almost every country of the world. This 'democratic international' must use many different methods, including industrial and military sabotage, labour agitation and strikes, continuous propaganda, terrorist acts against traitors and German leaders, boycotts and riots.

It is quite clear to me that an organisation on this scale and of this character is not something which can be handled by the ordinary departmental machinery of either the British Civil Service or the British Military Machine. What is needed is a new organisation to co-ordinate, inspire, control and assist the nationals of the oppressed countries who must themselves be the direct participants. We need absolute secrecy, a certain fanatical enthusiasm, willingness to work with people of different nationalities, complete political reliability. Some of these qualities are certainly to be found in some military officers and, if such men are available, they should undoubtedly be used. But the organisation should, in my view, be entirely independent of the war office machine."

Dr Dalton had completed his Doctorate at the London School of economics and worked as a barrister. He had served in the First World War and was awarded a medal for bravery by the Italian allies. Post war he had entered politics as a Labour MP and was a supporter of Winston Churchill in his stance against appeasement politics in dealing with the Nazis.

At the same time this process was unfolding, another source was also urging Churchill to create a separate subversive warfare organisation. Neville Chamberlain had resigned as Prime Minister on 10th July, the day Churchill was elevated to the post. Chamberlain as Prime Minister had been responsible for the politics of appeasement with which Britain and France had dealt with Hitler during the 1930s, resulting in Germany's expansion into Austria, Czechoslovakia and the invasion of Poland. After resigning Chamberlain maintained a position in government as Lord President of the Council, free of formal duties he had time to plan and propose matters such as this. With the authority of the Prime Minister he developed a draft policy which was finalised on the 19th July and this became the founding charter for SOE. Incidentally, this policy was the last thing Chamberlain did for his country as shortly afterwards he became ill and unable to serve further. He died of a stroke later that same year.

The policy gave Lord Swinton, who had set up the Home Defence (security) Executive to coordinate action against fifth columnists, executive control over MI5 and operational control over MI6. Paragraph 4 goes on to direct that, '*a new organisation shall be established to co-ordinate all action, by way of subversion and sabotage, against the enemy overseas*'. It then directs six actions to be taken including the name, Special Operations Executive, the three departments to be merged and those with control.

Lord Halifax took the findings of the meeting of 1st July to Churchill who on 16th July sent for Dalton and asked him to take ministerial charge of the new body for subversive warfare.

The three departments to be merged were:

1) D SECTION

This section had been formed in 1938 in the Secret Intelligence Service by Admiral Sir Hugh Sinclair, KCB who had secured the secondment of Major Lawrence Grand RE. The purpose was to study the possibilities of a British organisation for offensive action on the lines used by both Germany and Italy. Grand's recommendations included a list of possible sabotage targets inside Germany including, electrical supplies, telephone networks, food, ships, aeroplanes and agriculture. It also suggested organisations and individuals in Germany which could be used for sabotage such as communists, workers and Jews. It was suggested that neutral countries should be monitored for goods en route to Germany but no action to be taken in peace time. That immediate research should commence into sabotage devices, production of supplies, identification of targets and the organisation of depots and contacts in neutral countries.

2) ELECTRA HOUSE (E H)

The name is derived from the location of where the chairman of the Imperial Communications Advisory Committee, Sir Campbell Stuart, had his office. This office was set up in January 1939 with the purpose of the delivery of, quick and efficient conveyance of British news and views to potentially enemy people, in other words propaganda. This was seen as an area in need of co-ordination as a number of organisations had an interest in this area such as the BBC, Ministry of Information and most recently D Section.

Electra house was directed by the Foreign Office and the lack of co-ordination had led to problems at the beginning of the war when the BBC made complaints of conflicting direction from the Ministry of Information and EH. An early initiative of EH, in May 1940, was the development of the Freiheitsender (freedom station), a short wave radio transmitting messages and information purporting to be sent from within an enemy country.

An example of the sort of black propaganda expected was given on 28th October 1940. Time Magazine reported, "*Last week for the first time in six months CBS's short-wave listening post picked up a newscast aired by the celebrated German Freiheitsender—the secret 'Freedom Station' the Nazis have repeatedly tried to suppress. Giving no location, announcing simply that his program was 'Germany Speaking,' the Freiheitsender commentator, who may have been speaking from Switzerland, mocked Göring on the failure of his second four-year plan, which ended last week, contended Hitler had overrun Austria, Czechoslovakia, Poland, Denmark, Norway, the Low Countries and France because ersatz food and gasoline had failed him, declared the only people not weeping in Germany are the rascals*".

Electra house did not stay under the roof of SOE and was later transferred to the control of the Political Warfare Executive (PWE).

3) MILITARY INTELLIGENCE (RESEARCH) MI(R)

This department was first formed, in March 1938, under the title General Staff (Research) shortened to GS(R). The remit announced in the House of Commons was, *'to study the practice and lessons of actual warfare.'*

The War Office gave it a more specific remit, *'research into problems of tactics and organisation under the direction of DCIGS liaise with other branches of the W.O. and with other commands in order to collect new ideas on these subjects. Liaison with technical research branches'*. It was also given license to go where it liked, talk to who it liked, to remain anonymous and be kept from files, correspondence and phone calls.

In December 1938 Lt Col J.F.C. Holland, DFC, RE, was appointed as the head of department. He had previous experience of defence against irregular warfare in Ireland and India and produced a number of papers suggesting proposed courses of action. Following liaison with section D joint proposals recommended the development of defensive tactics, alternative to organised armed resistance, based on experiences in India, Iraq, Ireland and Russia. The proposals dealt with Romania, Denmark, Holland, Poland Bohemia, Austria, Germany, Libya and Abyssinia and suggested the department be expanded under Colonel Holland with 25 other officers and a budget of £500,000.

These proposals were accepted in principle by the Foreign Secretary and Colonel Holland's new department was formed in April 1939 in accommodation shared with section D. It was not until February 1940 that the department's final terms of reference were established and included the planning for projects involving irregular forces, technical research, operation of projects not undertaken by other departments of the War Office (WO), collection of information outside the remit of other MI departments and the interviewing and training of suitable personnel.

The above pre-war planning and arrangements show a clear mentality within both military and political circles of the inevitability of war with Germany and the extent to which this was going to be in both a geographical and ethical nature. Irregular warfare was not a new concept to the British; Edward III conducted a most unethical form (for the time) of fast moving, mounted, raiding war against the French who continued to try to fight him with tactics accepted by the chivalric code. During the First World War Lawrence of Arabia used similar tactics against the Turks.

From the start SOE experienced opposition for numerous reasons. The areas which SOE was to operate in overlapped the spheres of influence of other established departments. The concept of ungentlemanly warfare did not sit easily with military minds of more established professionals who often saw SOE as 'a bunch of interfering amateurs'. Those in the corridors of power felt SOE would undermine their personal power bases. The established intelligence services did not want another intelligence service operating in their areas and more importantly did not want the proactive actions proposed, as they believed this would stir up a hornets' nest and endanger their agents thus compromising their own work. Lastly Britain was not ready for conflict and following the recovery of the BEF from France the demand for resources was an issue which would be a problem throughout the war. In particular SOE had to fight for air and sea resources which were imperative to their ability to operate abroad.

In late 1940 the Air Ministry asked SOE to mount an operation into occupied France to intercept and kill the German pilots of a special 'Pathfinder' bomber section. This section, Kampfgeschwader 100, was based near Meucon in Brittany and the pilots were transported to their aircraft each night in the same transport vehicle. One of these aircraft had crash landed in Britain and the crew had given intelligence which had given birth to the idea that without these pilots the Luftwaffe bombers would be dropping their loads blind. At the time some Free French agents were being parachute trained at Ringway and permission was granted by General de Gaulle to use these agents for the mission. At this stage SOE had few staff, let alone trained agents and aircraft, and when the request was made for air transport to the Chief of Air Staff, Sir Charles Portal and head of Bomber Command, Sir Arthur Harris resisted and even tried to insist that any agents sent should be dressed in uniform as the Royal Air force could not be associated with any operation where the enemy were killed by men in civilian clothes. This was at a time where the Luftwaffe was indiscriminately bombing civilians in the London Blitz!

Bomber Harris was also very resistant to diverting resources away from his vision of how the war was going to be won. By both targeted bombing to incapacitate the German war effort and indiscriminate bombing of civilians thereby destroying the moral of the German population who would then revolt and usurp Hitler's regime. Incidentally he had the experience of the Blitz to draw on, which only hardened the resolve of the population of Britain to fight on and this is exactly the effect that Allied bombing of German cities had on the German population.

SIS would not share any of its training facilities with SOE as they believed that the amateurs would be captured very quickly and under interrogation give to the Germans valuable intelligence concerning SIS methods of operation, codes etc.

In July 1940 Hugh Dalton started to organise SOE from his office of the Ministry of Economic Warfare in Berkeley Square London and assumed the symbol SO as a codename. A chief executive officer (CEO) was appointed, also housed at Berkeley House, and was made responsible for the working of SOE as a whole. Offices at 64 Baker Street, London were allocated and given the cover name of Inter Services Research Bureau (ISRB). The head at this location was codenamed CD and in August Sir Frank Nelson, a former MP, took up this post until 1942. He was succeeded by Major General Colin Gubbins who held the post until the end of the war. The initial task was to bring together three separate bodies to function as one for a common cause.

The structure of D section was retained and the organisation was divided into sections with a responsibility for individual countries. Each Section had a head and the department was code-named with a letter, generally relating to the country in question, for instance for France, F Section. Throughout the war France remained a politically sensitive area and in total six sections was developed to deal with the issues involved. Some countries were encompassed within a regional section, The Americas U section, and Africa W section. For some countries the insignia letter did not relate, Germany X section and Italy J section. The ideal section head was fluent in the language, culture and history of their assigned nation, the same ideal was desired for all section members but not wholly achieved. The various sections were separated both in where they were accommodated and where they were trained for security reasons.

In the short time that SOE existed, the structure in respect of staffing levels, training, administration and logistical support grew to become huge, with the infrastructure of any long established organisation of a similar size. This is incredible, bearing in mind that the basic concept was that it was a secret organisation not talked about at any level, from Parliament to the most basic employee level. Recruitment was by invite or by such means as advertising for speakers of foreign languages with no further details given. The highest point for staff was around September 1944 at just under 13,000 this figure encompasses both men and women, military and non-military personnel. (The Secret History of SOE, Mackenzie).

Accommodation was required for offices, training, research, storage and personnel. In the area of Baker Street and across London, various office buildings were obtained for the country sections, but for training and research many stately homes all across Britain were obtained leading to the nickname for the organisation, 'Stately 'Omes of England'.

SOE was initially financed from secret funds to avoid explanations to outsiders; the financial director was Wing Commander

Venner whose final tally of SOE's cost was a profit of £23 million Pounds! All staff of the SOE payroll were classed as 'specially employed' and not remunerated from military funds and did not pay income tax. It is incredible that an organisation that employed so many people and sent out vast quantities of ordnance, munitions and stores to countries from France, Africa, The Balkans, Far East and Scandinavia can have run at a profit, but one example gives a flavour for the type of operations run to create such finance. Walter Fletcher was a European man, huge in stature, who worked as an international trader with a leaning towards the nefarious. He was commissioned to smuggle rubber out of the Japanese controlled Dutch East Indies. He wanted half a million Pounds to finance his exploits but was given £100,000. He failed to obtain any rubber in the Dutch East Indies and French Indo-China. After two years SOE was about to shut him down when he changed tactics and moved to mainland China. This area was a no go for SOE who had an agreement with OSS not to operate there. SOE, on Fletcher's request, supplied him with diamonds bought from De Beers and Swiss watches smuggled out of France by F section, both paid for with Sterling. Fletcher in turn sold these goods to Chinese magnates for their wives and mistresses at hugely inflated prices netting a total of £77 million.

Scientific research, development of weapons, explosive devices, equipment and agent training are large subjects and therefore will be dealt with as they relate to Desmond's story.

W SECTION – WEST AFRICA.

W Section was one of the first country sections to be formed by SOE and was instigated from an approach made by Walter Fletcher with an old Etonian friend Major Desmond Morton. Morton was a confident of Churchill and at the outbreak of war had joined the MEW and obviously was aware of the formation of SOE. At this time Fletcher was associated with a London firm dealing with rubber importations from around the Empire and lived on the fence between honesty and smuggling. Fletcher's plan was to target the French Colonies in West Africa and turn them to the Free French/Allied camp, thereby denying the Axis forces valuable war materials. The plan was complex and involved economic factors and propaganda methods needed to secure one or more colonies. The plan was obviously seen as good as it was adopted in principle as the basis for the Military Mission which was subsequently sent to West Africa. Fletcher was side lined but later used to great effect in another arena as previously described.

The person chosen to head this Military Mission was Louis Franck, codenamed W. Franck who was born in Belgium in 1908 to a famous banking family and in 1935 had moved to London for employment with the Merchant bankers, Samuel Montagu and Company. On the outbreak of war Franck joined the MEW and was regarded as a bullion expert. In September 1940 a Mission to Dakar was mounted by General de Gaulle in an effort to turn the West African colonies loyal to the Vichy regime to that of his Free French. Franck accompanied the mission which was a failure but he had developed a good relationship with de Gaulle and maintained that relationship after the mission. Franck initially set up his headquarters in Lagos at the end of 1940 and set about forming stations at the other three colonies. At this stage SOE and the PWE were still one entity, so his terms of reference were propaganda as well as subversive warfare, with the additional responsibility of intelligence gathering due to the lack of SIS presence in the region. The dangers to British interests in the region were not just the French; Spain and Portugal had interests in the region as well. In the summer of 1941 the mission was split into two, French West Africa (FRAWEST) under Lt Colonel Wingate and Neutral Colonies (NEUCOLS) under Franck. The latter clearly had a different strategic objective to the former but two notable coups were successful. The first was the corruption of the Captain of a Vichy ship, Gazcon, in Portuguese Lobito Bay in July 1941. For £10,000 the Captain brought his ship outside territorial waters where he was met by HMS Albatross. His cargo of castor seed and the ship had an estimated value of £400,000 to the British war effort. The second coup was in the harbour of the Spanish Island of Fernando Po, Operation Postmaster. An Italian Liner of 7,000 tons and two smaller German ships and their crews were berthed here in January 1942. One evening they were encouraged to attend a lavish party on shore and whilst away a party of 34 Englishmen constituted of 17 SOE agents (the rest being Nigerian civil servant volunteers), boarded the three vessels, captured the small enemy crews and sailed the ships to sea where they were then intercepted by HMS Violet.

On 11th August 1942 Desmond was interviewed for service with SOE. He had been recommended by GM which was the code for the head of W Section Colonel Louis Franck (HS 8/40), who also used the code W. He was interviewed by someone, presumably at the London headquarters of W Section, using the code WA. The identity of WA is elusive and appears on communication to London from West Africa, whilst it is dangerous to speculate as to who this code belonged to, it may well have been the section head's secretary or person responsible for administration. The first letter of a code was the section of SOE the operative belonged to and the second letter usually their area of responsibility, such as P for Politics, as in the code WP for Colonel G. Miles Clifford, W sections political advisor, or WE which was the code for Major R.E.C. Wingate responsible for Economics. In another section the person with the second letter of A was the section chief's secretary, possibly for administration.

Desmond was successful in his application and after signing the Official Secrets Act was re-employed immediately. On 22nd August 1942 he was transferred to the Intelligence Corps and allotted the number 7127 and the code W73 specifically employed as G.S.O.3 in the rank of Captain. The role of a General Service Officer 3 was split into three separate roles, intelligence, administration and operations. It is not stated which role Desmond was allotted to, but his role clearly involved the dissemination of intelligence reports and assuming he was GSO3 (i) his defined role from the manual of guidance of the day as supplied by the Intelligence Corps Museum was:

- *a) Co-ordination of all intelligence training and work of the division.*
- *b) Collection and collation of information about enemy positions, methods and intentions.*

c) *Daily intelligence summary.*
d) *Air photographs in conjunction with APIS (army photographic intelligence section) and air recce except artillery recce.*
e) *Liaison with APIS, field security officer and intelligence officers of HQ RA HQ RE and brigades*
f) *Press correspondents.*
g) *Handling of interpreters.*

The next definition given in this manual is that of IO's, Intelligence Officers and these are made subordinate to the GSO3 (1) so by assumption we can conclude that Desmond had a supervisory role of IO's.

The Intelligence Corps was formed in the First World War. The need for a distinct central intelligence gathering expertise recognised in the Boer War, prior to this Intelligence as a logistical support to military command was done on an ad hoc basis by individual commanders. During WW1 the use of radio and command and control communications systems were developed and as a counter measure the technique of locating and identifying enemy units by means of directional location equipment was developed. The Corps also effectively used civilian police drafted to military service as behind the lines detectors of enemy spies and to safeguard the integrity of lines of communication. Behind enemy lines activities were developed to glean information of troop movement, type and numbers. The interrogation of POWs was a role for specially trained officers and the smallest of details put together to create a larger picture of enemy strengths, likely locations of attack to develop defence and weak enemy areas to develop offensive strategies. For the interrogation end developing of information from civilian populations there was a definite desire to employ speakers of foreign languages. Another skill developed during World War One was the photographic interpretation unit. Aerial photographs of enemy displacement were taken both by hot air balloon and then by the Royal Flying Corps. At the end of the war the Corps was disbanded and by the start of World War Two there was a vacuum of staff trained to deliver the necessary intelligence for decision making at command level and the organisation was soon reformed to support the BEF. The reformed Corps grew to 3,040 officers and 5,930 other ranks and during this conflict the science of radio interception to gather evidence was exploited to the fullest. Approximately 40% of the personnel at Bletchley Park were Intelligence Corps staff.

On acceptance to SOE Desmond successfully completed courses in groups A and B.

TRAINING-GROUP A

Group A courses were known as Paramilitary Training or STS 21 and for many candidates were preceded by a week's preliminary training course at Wanborough Manor, STS 5 near Guildford, where their character and potential were assessed. Those deemed not suitable for employment by SOE were then taken to the 'cooler' where they were encouraged to forget all they had learnt. Many applicants knew nothing about SOE at this stage, as they had answered requests for foreign language speakers and nothing more. In Desmond's file there is no mention of a preliminary course or what duties he was engaged in between June and August 1942, but it is clear he knew of the existence of SOE by 11th August as his application form for employment was completed and signed in his handwriting. This form specifically requests employment within W Section and no doubt he had gained knowledge of SOE during his employment in the Congo. There is also the fact that he was recommended by the head of section, which may have negated the need for a course to determine his suitability. This application form also contains his own assessment of work he would be best suited to i.e. '*Liaison work with the Belgians or photographic work*'.

Those assessed suitable for further training were sent to the Arisaig area of Scotland near to Fort William on the Western Coast. The course was based at Arisaig House, a stately home with a long history dating back to Bonnie Prince Charlie. The house was commandeered by SOE for the purpose of agent training and given the code STS21. Its remoteness was ideal for the issue of security and maintaining the secret nature of the organisation and training. The house lies in 19 acres of wild Scottish highland and had 10 shooting lodges at various locations around the grounds. The staff and school were based in the main house and the pupils were housed in the shooting lodges. They were split by nationality or country section in keeping with policy, the less each agent knew the less the enemy could discover in the event of an agent falling into their hands.

The course at the time Desmond attended STS 21 was three weeks in duration, catered for 70 students at a time and was extremely gruelling, taking full advantage of the rugged terrain to test fitness and determination to survive and succeed. The course was later lengthened to five weeks. The curriculum involved tuition in;

1. Physical training
2. Silent killing
3. Weapons handling
4. Demolition
5. Map and compass reading
6. Field craft
7. Elementary Morse Code
8. Raid tactics

Two of the instructors are good examples of SOE's ability to recruit outside of the military box, thereby getting the best available talent for their purposes. William Fairbairn and Eric Anthony Sykes, two ex-Shanghai municipal police officers, who taught the art of close quarter combat and silent killing. The two men had learnt their trade in the world of Chinese gangs in the streets of Shanghai and had developed a killing knife which bears their name, the Fairbairn-Sykes Commando knife; this weapon became the trademark of the British Commando forces.

In modern parlance the knife would be described as an offensive weapon per se i.e. built specifically for causing injury. The handle is ribbed to prevent the user's hand slipping on the victim's blood, creating self-inflicted injuries and the blade is pointed and slender for one purpose, stabbing. It does not have a cutting edge and has no other practical use. It gives a clear picture of the experience these two officers had in the nefarious underworld and therefore of their qualification to teach these skills.

Handgun firearms training also bore the trademark of these two men who had developed a technique for firing a pistol from the hip at close quarters. The gun holding hand elbow was tucked tightly into the waist and the firer pointed their body at the target, two shots were fired called a double tap. The system was later adopted by American forces and parts are still used in police firearms training to this day.

Fairbairn was a student to a high degree of boxing and various martial arts and his body was covered in scars from knife fights on the streets of Shanghai. He was employed as an officer and rose to the rank of Lieutenant Colonel during the war and was known as 'Dangerous Dan'.

Explosives training was also taught on this course and the West Highland rail line cooperated with facilities to lay dummy charges on actual railway lines and provided the school with a train. Exercises were held whereby agents had to get to a certain location at night, for dummy charges to be laid in time for the passing of a particular train and then get back to the school without being caught by the local police.

TRAINING-GROUP B

Group B courses were also called, Finishing School or STS 31 and the lessons taught here were to give the agents skills in the field to live in enemy occupied territory and avoid capture. Accommodation for this school was found in the stately home residence of Lord Montagu at Beaulieu in the New Forest near Southampton. The palace home has its origin in the 13th century when it was the great gatehouse for Beaulieu Abbey. On the dissolution of the Abbeys in 1538 the house was bought by Sir Thomas Wriosthesley, later to become the first Earl of Southampton and has remained in the Montagu family ever since. The grounds of the home are extensive, remote and again perfect for the purpose sought from both security and secretive aspects. They also contained many other houses which were used for student accommodation and the students were again kept segregated by nationality and section for security reasons. There were 11 schools within the complex and each school had five sections covering such topics as:

1. Agent technique, clandestine life, personal security, communication in the field, how to maintain a cover story and how to act under police surveillance
2. Practical appliance of the above skills
3. Knowledge of enemy forces
4. Propaganda
5. Codes and ciphers

Other areas covered were disguises, use of invisible ink, burglary, lock picking and safe breaking. Agents were permanently compromised if their identity papers fell into the wrong hands, giving the Gestapo a photograph of the person they wanted and SOE had Harley Street plastic surgeons available to change an agent's appearance if needed. A German Jewish volunteer had a facial transformation to allow him to be dropped into Germany without being visibly identifiable as a Jew.

Agents were constantly tested for ability and security; if they fell into the hands of the local police they were furnished with an emergency telephone number to use as a last resort, but were more highly thought of for brazening out their predicament. Female officers were used to test potential agents, allowing themselves to fall into the company of off duty agents and testing whether they would be indiscreet or not. To this end bedrooms were bugged with listening devices giving a clear indication that life at Beaulieu was a constant test but not altogether unrewarding!

WEST AFRICA

Desmond sailed for Africa on 29th September 1942 and arrived on the West Coast on 17th October.

British West Africa consisted of four colonies, Sierra Leone, Gold Coast, Gambia and Nigeria. The political map of West Africa below shows the British territories in pink with a red border and the French territories in purple. Following the fall of France all of this French Territory was loyal to the Vichy Regime except for the area between Nigeria and the Congo (French Equatorial Africa), which became Free French and loyal to General de Gaulle.

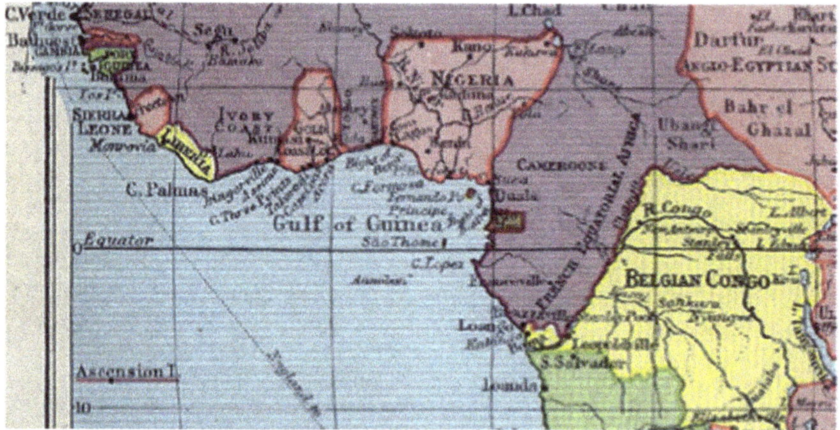

Political map of Africa 1940 (courtesy of Probert Encyclopaedia)

Sierra Leone is very rich in a multitude of mineral resources including diamonds, gold, titanium, bauxite and rutile. Freetown is the capital which is situated on the southern mouth of the world's third largest natural harbour, Queen Elizabeth II Quay. This harbour was the base of the Royal Navy's South Atlantic Command and became a major rallying point for convoys. On this occasion Desmond left the convoy at the changeover point of Freetown and travelled to Gambia where he commenced his duties of GSO 3 at the Bathurst station. He was stationed at this location for six months and for two of them he acted as the head of section.

Gambia was the first and also the last West African British Colony, from 1856 to 1965. It is a country greatly dependent on agriculture and its economy is dominated by farming, fishing and now tourism. In the planning stages for W Section Louis Franck was asked if Gambia should be defended in the event of an attack by Vichy forces as it was very small and surrounded by French colonies which had large forces. The Colonial Office considered Bathurst pivotal in the communications network with the other British Colonies and any plans to abandon it without a fight were dropped.

On 2nd May 1943 Desmond was transferred to the Freetown station at Sierra Leone where he was the head of section until he departed for the UK on 5th November 1943.

Unfortunately, few files and records have survived concerning SOE's activities in West Africa and Desmond's personal file gives no clues as to his specific activities other than he was employed in an administrative role, but it does intimate he went on missions. Family records reveal no clues and all Desmond's Africa memorabilia appears to be dated from his time in the Congo, even the Africa map where he detailed his travels in line form, have not been updated to show his whereabouts in Sierra Leone or Gambia. W73 followed his training in secrecy and left no clues.

The situation in West Africa is, however, an excellent example of the difficulties faced by SOE in the face of their opponents and the potential conflicts between SOE's *raison d'etre* and the interests of military command and politics. The four British colonies were surrounded by French territories, most of which were loyal to the Vichy government; therefore the British were surrounded by hostile forces.

British interests in the region were controlled by the Colonial Office whose responsibility was to administer the colony, make it self-funding and at the same time create extra produce to be sent back to Britain. The military commander for the region was responsible for the defence of the colonies. Both had every reason to suppose that to allow SOE a free hand to follow their directives and create mayhem in the Vichy territories would be counter-productive to the profitability and security of the British colonies.

At the outbreak of war West Africa was largely divided between France and Britain, the two former German colonies, Togo and Cameroon, given to the French by the Treaty of

Versailles. There was no intelligence gathering mechanism and spying between the two main nations had stopped many years before. On the fall of France and before the Vichy Government was formed, talks were held between Pierre Laval and Hitler, where the former had actually suggested that a joint French and German force invade the British Colonies in West Africa. Events such as these had created a real fear of invasion in the region and by 1942 the official Colonial Office policy was not to provoke the Vichy regimes, therefore SOE had an invaluable role in intelligence gathering, but a curbed role in respect of their disruptive duties. This had caused much frustration on behalf of the SOE W section leadership and surely for the agents who had undergone extensive training and then found they could not use their acquired skills.

By October 1942 the political and military situations had stabilised and remained static until the Allied invasion of North Africa, when Vichy forces made little effort to resist, the only fighting was over in three days.

Desmond's previous service in the Belgian Congo had prepared him for his role with W section. His extensive travels throughout Africa had given him the education needed to accept his administrative role of assessing and grading intelligence reports gathered by field agents. Whilst much of the records of SOE's work has been lost or destroyed, one colony, the Gold Coast, had retained many records marked for destruction which has given a picture of what was happening across the region. The agricultural nature of the region meant that there was some nomadic movement across borders by farmers and traders. Some of these people were recruited to spy on the Vichy colonies and return with intelligence for which they were paid. The sort of information gathered varied in quality and the grading of such was Desmond's role.

It is the smallest jig-saw pieces of information which can be used to give a picture of the enemy for military command, for example, the number of toilet rolls ordered in a given period gives an accurate estimation of troop numbers at a given location. This information can be gleaned from a number of sources;

railway employees, civilian delivery drivers, cleaners, store personnel or even enemy store-men. Desmond's role here was the grading of the information by type and source and the onward dissemination dependent on the quality and importance.

Desmond's personal file simply states; "*Whilst with these sections he carried out administrative duties and gathered SOE intelligence in respect of the territories under his control*".

It also states, "*He has fulfilled his duties very satisfactorily whilst with this section*".

Also on file at this stage are comments by W.S.

Off the record impression by W.S. On 7127.

"*This officer is a gunner who has, I believe, been away from active duty ever since the beginning of the war. He has been on missions, one or another, both in SOE and out of it. His French is good. He is a very pleasant social type but does not allow his work to interfere with his other pursuits. I think he would do extremely well if he was given a course of discipline both physical and mental, probably with his own regiment*".

(Author's note; This 'off the record' observation forms part of Desmond's official SOE record which to those enlightened in the age of Freedom of Information will not make sense).

Unfortunately there are no records to determine what the above mentioned missions referred to, but these comments were noted in a later appraisal of his activities when awards were being determined.

On 5th November 1943 Desmond departed the shores of West Africa and returned to the UK; the journey taking 20 days indicating he travelled by sea.

PART V

FRANCE AND RF SECTION

FRENCH SECTIONS

Following the fall of France in 1940, there developed a very tangled and difficult situation in French/British politics. The Vichy Government was a collaborator with the enemy, but initially a desire was retained to maintain open communications with them in an effort to obtain their co-operation with respect to the colonies, resources from the colonies and resistance and intelligence inside France. The French Forces which escaped to Britain fought for recognition as the Free French and in particular General de Gaulle who sought recognition as the lawful leader of France in exile. De Gaulle appears to be an abrasive character who did not suffer being side-lined when it came to anything to do with his homeland, but it is clear he had the current and future interests of France at heart. This is evidenced in a War Cabinet document circulated to the Prime Minister, War Cabinet and Defence Committee by the Secretary of the War Cabinet Mr E.E. Bridges on 7th August 1943. The Document's header is '*An outline of relations between His Majesty's Government and General de Gaulle between June 1940 and June 1943*'. This document details the relationship between General de Gaulle and the British establishment and the efforts made by the latter to accommodate him in the recognition and setting up of a Free French Council in Britain and support for his failed mission to West Africa to attempt to persuade the Vichy Regimes there to support his Free French cause. It catalogues a series of disputes, which amounted to belligerence or ingratitude on behalf of de Gaulle, which led to deterioration in relationships during this period. De Gaulle continually complained of lack of cooperation and that his recruiting efforts were continually frustrated by a lack of comprehension by British officers and officials. Winston Churchill intervened and resolved problems on many occasions. This is a very interesting document giving a clear picture of the events of the period and the relationship between Britain and the Free French at many levels.

Originally the section set up by SOE to deal with resistance in France was F Section, but without the knowledge of de Gaulle, as Winston Churchill did not like or trust him. De Gaulle was not happy when he found out that the British Intelligence Services were developing interests in France without his knowledge and permission and therefore a separate section was set up to deal solely with the Free French supporters of de Gaulle. The situation in France, with respect to developing resistance movements, was largely based on opposing political views and Communists were setting up groups separately to supporters of de Gaulle sometimes with disastrous results from lack of cooperation. The Communist groups were always very suspicious of British motivations and whilst gladly accepted support in arms, munitions, finance etc. could not be relied upon to accept British directions, choosing to take their lead from Russia. In total five sections were formed to deal with aspects of France including the escape routes for airmen, the Polish community and an office in Algiers to deal with the South of the country.

F Section remained under British control and dealt with all groups not supporting de Gaulle whilst RF Section was jointly run by Britain and General de Gaulle's Free French Forces. General de Gaulle, with the cooperation of the British Government, set up a council for the defence of France overseas and on 7th August 1940 this council was given legal status in a memorandum issued by Winston Churchill. The council then set up a Free French Intelligence Service and named it the Central de Renseigements et d'Action or BCRA and was led by Commandant (Major) Andre Dewavrin codenamed Colonel Passy. RF section and the BCRA worked in close cooperation. The BCRA headquarters was situated near to the Baker Street home of RF Section, at 10 Duke Street.

With the planning well under way at SHAEF for the creation of a second front and the invasion of Europe, SOE, the American OSS and the BCRA were tasked with organising missions to France, Belgium and Holland to organise and supply resistance networks in support of the invasion. A number of units were developed to achieve this aim; the SAS were to send fighting units and the SOE were to develop two basic units, Jedburgh teams and Inter-Allied Missions.

- Jedburgh teams were three man units sent to an area of enemy territory where there were known established resistance groups. Their missions were to direct operations as dictated by Allied HQ in direct support the invasion, organise the delivery of arms and equipment, train and support the resistance units in reception and use of the arms. The teams were a mixture of British, American and French personnel, two officers one of whom was the commander, and a radio operator NCO.
- The Inter-Allied units were similar to the Jedburghs in objectives and multi-national make-up, but were not restricted to three members; their sphere of operations was in areas where there were no known established resistance groups.

TRANSFER

On 27th November 1943 Desmond attended an interview for transfer to RF Section of SOE. The interviewing officer was Squadron Leader, later to be Wing Commander F.F.E. Yeo-Thomas G.C. At this interview it was apparent that Desmond had domestic issues and Yeo-Thomas tried to persuade him to withdraw his application for this most hazardous work. Desmond was not to be dissuaded and persisted with his application; he was successful and was transferred the same day to SOE RF section agents list. The interview was designed to test not only the applicant's command of French, but also the individual's self-discipline and resolve, There were very good reasons to fail Desmond, but it is an accolade to his character and resolve that he was perceived to be of such value. Successful applicants to SOE were a rare breed of men and women and the selection processes at all stages were designed to retain only the very best.

Yeo-Thomas was the deputy head of RF section and not a man to suffer fools gladly. On the day he interviewed Desmond he saw a total of eight candidates and accepted only two. This is an indicator to assess that even during the great need of war and in particular the imminent invasion of Europe that standards required of potential agents were high and were not a casualty of expediency. Yeo-Thomas himself had already completed two successful missions to France organising resistance movements for the Free French forces under the command of General de Gaulle. He was from a British family who had lived in France for some time and worked before the war in Paris for the famous fashion house of Molyneux. When France was invaded he escaped to England and swore to return and help liberate the country he loved. Initially he joined the RAFVR and was turned down for flight duties due to his age; he was instead used as an interpreter. On gaining a commission he was then employed as an intelligence officer for a Polish squadron where he made friends with George Whitehead, a Polish born Englishman who was with the same squadron as an interpreter. Yeo-Thomas found his way to SOE and progressed to be deputy head of RF Section. He was a determined and forthright man who was not afraid to buck the system for his beliefs and found himself one day before Winston Churchill with a few minutes to impress the great man with what he needed. He succeeded in impressing the Prime Minister and the French resistance benefited with greater resources of both aerial transport and arms. Whilst Yeo-Thomas was pursuing his quest which led to this interview, he was frustrated by constant obstacles and bureaucracy and during this difficult time Desmond became a great source of support and a friendship developed, that was later of huge benefit to both men. George Whitehead was also a big support to Yeo-Thomas and the three men's destinies were to be entwined.

The domestic issues which are hinted at in the various sources including Desmond's SOE personal file (pf) was simply that following the birth of their third child, Jacquie, Margaret suffered post-natal depression. A common enough illness and treated these days with a greater level of understanding and sensitivity, but in these times of national crisis and lesser medical understanding, Margaret was subjected to electric shock therapy which caused irreparable damage and sadly she was unable to look after her children. Desmond's SOE pf was marked with a note that in the event of anything happening to him, Margaret was not to be informed in the first instance and that any approach to the family should be made via his parents, who would be able to break any bad news at an appropriate time.

TRAINING

Desmond commenced a period of training and in December 1943 he successfully completed a parachute training course at STS 51 the Ringway near Manchester. Students were housed in Dunham House (STS51a) where they also completed the theory associated with the course. Much of the science of parachute descent was developed by SOE as part of their scientific development programme. Students underwent an intensive physical exercise programme and then had to complete a minimum of two jumps, one from a static balloon and one from an aeroplane. They were equipped with a small spade attached to a leg with which they buried the parachute and jump suit on landing. Operational Jumps were often from low level between 300 to 400 feet to avoid radar detection. From this altitude the jumper will hit the ground after 10-15 seconds so the 'chute was operated automatically by a static line 'hooked up' inside the aeroplane. Desmond's final report from this course is as follows:

' "*An excellent student who worked hard throughout the course. He was apparently unaccustomed to a great deal of exercise as after the preliminary training he stiffened up and found a certain amount of difficulty in getting around, however, he recovered from this and made four good descents by day. At first his landings were a little unorthodox but he quickly conquered this and completed his last two descents in perfect style, the last in quite a high wind. He received lectures on containers and disposal and reception committee working. A very good type who (unreadable) through the course with the exception of the night descent in a quiet and efficient style. Although somewhat out of condition he improved physically quickly and there seems little doubt he will prove an excellent subject. Four descents; first class.*

It is a shame that the surviving record is damaged as it would appear Desmond did not complete a night jump which was essential for the insertion to enemy territory by parachute. It speaks volumes about his determination and character that, although he was not a young soldier and he had spent a comfortable war so far in Africa, he chose to leave that lifestyle behind, compete in an environment where many fitter younger men would fall short and succeed with a highly praising report!

He then attended a course at STS 40, Howbury Hall near Waterend, Bedford which taught the use and maintenance of S-Phone and Eureka sets and also more input in Reception Committee procedure. The S-Phone and Eureka sets were communication equipment between agents on the ground and aircraft locating a drop zone. A pre-agreed recognition letter was transmitted from the ground to let the aircrew know that all was well and the drop could go ahead. The S-Phone operator on the ground then directed the pilot to the correct location.

Desmond's end of course report is dated 6th January 1944 and makes the following observations:

> ' "*S-Phone, has a thorough knowledge of the S-Phone. Eureka, Good pass, capable of operating and maintaining Eureka sets. R.C. work, Has shown great enthusiasm and has a good knowledge of the subject. C.O. remarks; a keen and capable officer.*"

On 23rd February RF section was advised by A/CD that approval was given for Desmond to be committed to a mission in the field.

Desmond also completed a course at STS 39 Hackett School; in Subversive Propaganda, this was where agents, who had shown a flare for the subject at Finishing School, were taught about the use and distribution of propaganda which is split into three distinctive areas; black, grey and white. Black propaganda is mostly based on lies and false information and delivered to the target in such a way that the recipients do not know the true source. An example of this technique was used in 1943 and involved the making of German postage stamps which displayed the head of Reichsführer-SS Heinrich Himmler instead of that of Hitler, the purpose was to hide the origin and enhance the rumour already instigated that the SS was planning a coup to usurp Hitler.

Grey Propaganda was a mixture of truth and lies but again delivered in a way to disguise the true origins. The PWE set up a powerful radio transmitter in an underground bunker near Crowborough, Sussex and transmitted messages under the guise of being a German radio station named Soldatensender Calais. The main target for these transmissions was the German U-Boat fleet and transmitted music, sporting updates and anything thought to be of interest to German sailors. These truths were interspersed with lies such as, conmen fleecing soldiers being transferred to the Eastern front and anything likely to cause a drop in moral. The transmissions were sent out between 6 p.m. and dawn and the presenter was Agnes Bernelle using the code-name, 'Vicky'.

White Propaganda is the truth, delivered in a way designed to identify the true source, for example, the BBC transmitted many messages of encouragement to the occupied countries giving information concerning the Nazi regime and obviously did not hide the source.

Hackett School was originally formed by D Section in 1940 under the direction of Kim Philby (later exposed as a Russian mole within the British Intelligence Service). Philby was joined by Major J Hackett in 1941 a former advertising executive and the school re-named accordingly. The school was jointly run by SOE and the PWE and by the time Desmond attended his course, in May 1944, the school was located near Aldenham at a stately home called Wall Hall. This was the war time residence of the US Ambassador to Britain, Joseph P Kennedy Sr. Whilst on this course Desmond made the acquaintance of Sgt. Peter Wall-Gray who was employed in STS 39 due to his photographic skills. Wall-Gray had worked for Kodak before the war and was a member of the Territorial Army. Called up at the commencement of hostilities, he was originally assigned to a Search Light Unit, as had Desmond, which was another point they had in common as well as a passion for photography. Wall-Row's expertise in the photographic development art had been enhanced by military training and he had transferred to STS 37, Beaulieu, in 1943 from a specialist camouflage development and training unit. At Beaulieu he was employed to take agent photographs and helped in the development of advanced photography including microphotography. Wall-Row's role in STS39 was the development of posters, leaflets and photographs designed to undermine the moral of enemy troops depicting such things as SS troops having a good time with women back home in Germany, inferring to the troops that their wives or girlfriends were being unfaithful whilst they were at the front.

The report following Desmond's successful completion of the course reads:

> *"26.5.44. Extremely promising student may be relied on to obtain results under field conditions."*

Desmond also received instruction in parachute container packing. This course was STS 61 at Audley End, Saffron Waldon. The course is not listed on Desmond's SOE pf but it is safe to assume that an agent in the field would need a level of knowledge on what can be packed into a container for the purposes of ordering supplies. The fact that he received this instruction is gleaned from the record of his identity check questions and answers. One of the questions to be asked of him to verify that he was the genuine person on the radio and not a German replacement in the event of his capture is:

"Q. Where did you train with Major Cardozo?
A. S.T.S.61.

The other identity check questions were:

Q. *What port in Africa did you work in?*
A. *Freetown.*
Q. *Whose flat did you go to for contacts in North France and Belgium?*
A. *Major Thackwaite's."*

These questions and answers were agreed before the start of a mission and recorded at SOE HQ to be used to verify the identity of anyone purporting to be the agent in question.

Major Thackwaite was the British member of inter-allied mission 'Union', whose role was to enter France to select and organise resistance in the area of Haute Savoie, France in the Vercors Plateau. This mission was a huge success with 3,000 resistants being recruited, trained, armed and causing problems for the German forces following D-Day.

Major Cardozo was an interesting character, of Portuguese descent his family moved to London in the later part of the 17th century and were involved in the tobacco trade. His father distinguished himself in World War One and Frederick Henry Cardozo was born in 1916. He became a professional soldier himself and during World War two joined SOE as he was a fluent French speaker. He parachuted into the Claremont-Ferrand area a few days after D-Day with exactly the same mission as Desmond. Frederick had a distinguished career in France and was awarded the MC, the Chevalier de la Légion d'honneur and the Croix de Guerre avec Palme. He survived the war and continued in his military career until retirement and died in 2011. From written testimony of him he appears very similar to Desmond in personality and became much revered by the French resistance due to his fluent French, bravery, organisational abilities and leadership skills.

MISSION ASSIGNMENT

Initially on being transferred to RF section, Desmond was assigned to support the established Rover circuit. A card has survived which records details of instructions given to Desmond for an insertion to Tarbes.

DENYS see HUBBLE D.E. CAPT R.A.

M. DENYS,	HTE. PYRENEES
Bijoutier,	Postbox for:-
Place de L'Eglise	ROVER/JULIEN
Tarbes.	Real name: C.T. RECHEMANN
	Known in this country as:
	C.T. RAYMOND

Instructions: Ask for Robert.

Password: "Ave-vous trios alliances en platine?"
"Non je n'en avais que deux en or fix."

(signed; Buckmaster)

REPRODUCTION OF FILING CARD IN HS9/756/1

'Postbox' was a term for a location where information could be collected and left for collection. In this case it was a jewellery shop and the coded greeting was to ask for three platinum wedding rings with the response that there were only two in gold.

Charles Théophile Rechenmann, code name Julien, was a captain in F section SOE. He was the founder of the Rover circuit, based in the area of Tarbes a city near to the Pyrenees Mountains South West France. Charles was a Frenchman from Moselle in the disputed Lorraine area and when the Germans invaded he was arrested but released in 1940. He was recruited to SOE in 1942 and given the task of organising a resistance movement in Tarbes. This he did using fellow Frenchmen from the Lorraine area but on 12th May he met René Boquereau, a resistance leader, at the Hotel du Cheval de Bronze in Angoulême. They were both arrested as Boquereau was working for the Gestapo and had denounced Rechenmann. He was interrogated by the Gestapo and subsequently taken to Fresnes Prison and then to Buchenwald. Boquereau continued to work with the Gestapo who attempted to arrange for more agents and arms be dropped but the subterfuge was discovered and Desmond was not despatched and transferred to Mission Citronelle.

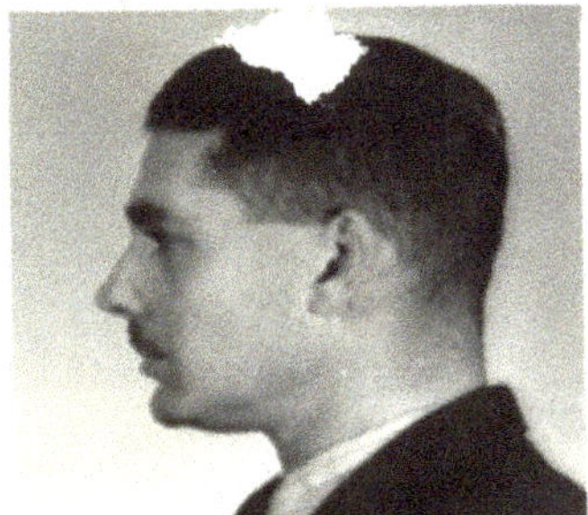

Desmond photographed in French attire and for his Alain Denys papers (National Archives)

PART VI

INTER-ALLIED MISSION CITRONELLE

MISSION CITRONELLE MEMBERS

Mission Citronelle was an Inter-Allied Mission devised by SOE and the BCRA to operate in the Ardennes area of France, in support of the D-Day landings in Normande. The original team for Citronelle was formed in January 1944 and consisted of Commandant Bollardière, First Lieutenant Victor Layton of the OSS, and Desmond as full members, with Flight Lieutenant George Whitehead RAF as an associate member.

Citronelle Stage I (11th April 1944).				
Name	**Field Name**	**Name used for Maquis**	**Name on false I.D. papers**	**Mission Role**
Jacques de Bollardière	Prisme	Commandant Prisme Monsieur Jacques	Jacques Petit	Commander
Victor Layton	TRIEDRE	Lieutenant Victor	Victor Launier	Quartermaster
Gérard Brault	SÉNÉGALAIS	Lieutenant Pierre	Pierre Boisson	Radio Operator

Citronelle Stage II (5th-6th June 1944).				
Desmond Ellis Hubble	Bissectrice	Capitaine Alain	Alain Denys	
George Whitehead	PARABOLE	Capitaine Georges	Georges Wilmart	Admin. Officer
Jacques Chavane	POINT	Capitaine Jacques	Maurice Charrière	Intelligence officer
Lucien Goetghebeur	Échardonnette	Lieutenant Lucien Bouboule	Lucien Bourbier	Sabotage Instructor
Gérard Racine	Brabant	Lieutenant Marc	Marc Brabant	Sabotage Instructor

Commandant Bollardière

Jacques Pâris de Bollardière
(Alias - Col. Prisme)

Photo Courtesy of M. Philippe LeClerc

Jacques Paris de Bollardière was born on December 16th 1907 at Châteaubriant, Loire, France. From a professional military family, he followed his father after college to the military academy at La Flèche and then to the École Spéciale Militaire de Saint-Cyr (special military school of Saint-Cyr) in 1927. He proved to be a very bad student, unruly and rebellious and he finished what should have been a two year course after a third year imposed as a punishment. He also graduated without honours with 'sardines' (French military nickname for sergeant insignia) instead of officers 'stripes'.

His first posting as a sergeant was to the 146th Infantry Regiment at St Avoid where he was subsequently promoted to Sous Lieutenant and posted to the 173rd RIA Bastia, where he was promoted full Lieutenant in October 1932. He was bored by garrison life and transferred to the French Foreign Legion in February 1935, where he was posted to the 1st Regiment based at Sidon, Algeria. The following year he transferred to the 4th Infantry Regiment where he continued to serve until February 1940, when he was assigned to 13th Demi-Brigade of the Foreign Legion (13th DBLE) and promoted to Captain.

When German forces invaded Norway, Britain and France sent forces to resist the invasion and assist Norway and Bollardière led his company in action until the invasion of France when he was withdrawn to Brest. A powerless witness to the overrunning of his country, he took the initiative and escaped to London on June 17th, in a trawler before General de Gaulle made the call to do so. He arrived in London two days later and joined the Free French Forces keeping his assignment with the 13th DBLE, 1st Free French Division. This division was engaged in campaigns in Eritrea and Gabon, East Africa where on 13th April 1941 he led his company of 90 men at the battle of Massawa and for this action he was awarded the Croix de la Libération.

In September 1941 he was promoted to Commandant (Major) of the 1st Battalion, French Foreign Legion posted to Libya. On 23rd October 1942 The battle of El Alamein commenced and the 1st Free French Brigade, commanded by General Koenig, were assigned the task of taking the heights of El Quartet Himeimat, a peripheral position held by Italian forces. It was logistically a difficult assault commanded by Bollardière with vehicles becoming stuck in the soft sand and the troops having to get to positions on foot, exhausted. Bollardière was seriously wounded in the arm by an exploding mine and withdrawn from the battle, spending eight months in hospital in Cairo. The wound not fully healed when he re-joined his command on 15th June 1943 at Sousse, Tunisia. It was here that he expressed his desire to take the fight back to French Soil and in November 1943 he returned to England to commence training in the BCRA intelligence service and was assigned the name Jacques Treffonds. He completed a parachute jump course, use of weapons and explosives, British, American and German. His course final report reads:

> *"He is intelligent and of practical mind, but not academic and maybe a little strict. His head is on his shoulders, has good judgement and is insightful and clever. Enthusiastic worker, volunteer, he has exceptional command arrangements. With a strong character, determined, loyal and reliable, He is sure of himself but not to excess, he has a pleasant personality, rather reserved. He is nevertheless very consensual, and should enjoy a high popularity among his comrades. He is a born leader who inspires confidence in his immediate subordinates. He seems well qualified to occupy a position of trust and authority, especially in delicate operations."*

Following successful completion of all his training he was assigned as Commander of Citronelle.

1st Lieutenant Victor Layton

Photo Courtesy of M. Philippe LeClerc

Born on 28th November 1921 in Vienna to Arthur and Margaret Lustig, Layton lived in this city until he was seven, as his father worked at the Bank of Central European Countries. The family then moved to Paris where he became fluent in French and in 1936 he was sent to England to continue his studies. He completed his studies in England and returned to France. At the outbreak of World War Two he made his way on false papers to Spain. In early 1941 Layton boarded a Portuguese ship bound for the USA; he landed at Hoboken, New Jersey and went to New York to continue his studies. He became an American citizen and changed his Germanic name to Layton. Whilst Germans were not treated as severely as Japanese following Pearl Harbour, there was still a great suspicion of anyone of German descent and the FBI had great successes against German spy networks.

In September 1942 he joined the US army Corps of Engineers as an officer and then was recruited to the OSS in June 1943 due to his fluency in French, German and English. He was sent to London to join SOE and in early 1944 assigned to Citronelle.

LIEUTENANT BRAULT

Gerard Brault was born on 29th April 1922 in Paris, of Senegalese ancestry. At the outset of war Brault is believed to be amongst a group of 800 plus young Frenchmen evacuated to England aboard a Belgian ship the Prince Leopold, which was then turned into an infantry landing ship by the Royal Navy. They were initially housed in London's Olympia Stadium and were addressed there by General de Gaulle, who was on a recruiting drive to enlarge the Free French Forces in Britain and abroad. Many of these young men volunteered and were inducted into the Free French Army and some were also chosen for special duties. What is certain is that whilst in London Brault volunteered to serve in the Free French Forces and on 30th June 1940 was attached to the 1st Airborne Infantry Company as a private. He undertook parachute and radio operator training and attended STS 38, Inchmery House (part of the Beaulieu Finishing School sometimes referred to as STS 36 in French sources), where he underwent and successfully completed paramilitary training. His training also included an extremely tough Commando course in the Bournemouth and Southampton areas of Southern England. Sometime in August 1941 Brault was amongst a group of trainees, who whilst training at Inchmery House, put on a display involving explosives for General de Gaulle. During this period Inchmery House was exclusively used by French RF section and BCRA agents and it had a reputation for superior food. This of course made it a sought after location amongst British agents also training in the Beaulieu complex, to visit and enjoy the French hospitality, whilst taking the opportunity to improve their French.

On 1st June 1941 Brault was assigned to the BCRA and on the night of 3rd June 1942, as part of Operation Crab, he parachuted into the area of Montluçon, Central France as a radio operator. The objectives of this operation were to encourage and enlist resistants in the region under the command of Jean Moulin and also to train and equip them appropriately to their needs. Jean Moulin's secretary, Jean Cordier, wrote about Brault's actions during the course of this mission: "*he alone managed to maintain communication lines with London HQ and often ignored his own safety by transmitting for up to six hours a day.*"

On 15th October 1942 a raid was mounted by 12 Gestapo agents accompanied by three French police officers and he was arrested whilst transmitting. Brault was fortunate to be detained in a French prison at Castres and with the help of a young Alsatian guard of the prison, M. Roschbach, managed to effect his escape on 29th June. On the night of 24th July, after being on the run, Brault was picked up from a field in Saint-Vulbas near Lyon and flown back to London.

Following a long period of leave, and time at the radio operator's school as an instructor, he was assigned to Citronelle.

FLIGHT LIEUTENANT WHITEHEAD

George Whitehead was born in Poland in December 1908 to an English family whose roots, via his paternal grandmother's side, lay in the Bradford area of England. The family were industrialists who had invested and prospered in the woollen trade during the time of the Industrial Revolution of Britain. The family had expanded their industrial interests to Poland and Russia and although were mainly permanently based in Poland, they maintained their English status by sending their children to public school in England. George was sent to Oundle School near Peterborough, which as one of the largest and most prestigious public schools, was formed by Sir William Laxton by endowment to the Worshipful Company of Grocers in 1556. Following a sound preparatory education at Oundle George he then attended Oxford University until 1931.

After leaving university in 1931 George spent five years mainly living in France with relatives where he became fluent in the French language and culture. He then returned to Poland to complete his obligation to National Service and spent one year in the Polish army.

He then entered the family business which survived the Great Depression of the 1920s and 30s and the Russian invasion of Poland, which was halted by Polish forces a matter of a few miles from the family's industrial complexes. George was tasked to develop the family interests in America and in 1939 he attended a trade fair in New York. The day he arrived, the Nazis entered and occupied Prague as part of Hitler's expansionist plans, allowed by Britain and France's policy of appeasement.

George immediately left America by ship to Genoa (the Americans had stopped sending ships to the countries in conflict); where from there he managed to continue to France where his two brothers had travelled also and enlisted in the RAF. He continued to England and volunteered for military service with the army but was told the RAF were badly in need of his linguistic skills, as Polish squadrons were being assembled and communication with the Poles was a huge problem. He was accepted for service, commissioned almost immediately and posted to Blackpool. He was then posted to the 308th Free Polish Fighter Squadron, stationed at RAF Bagington, near Coventry. He delayed travelling for a few days, which was fortunate, as the hotel he was to be billeted in was bombed and that would have been the end for him. At this stage RAF Bagington was a field with a few huts, which served as officers' and pilots' rest rooms, with the mess being a tent serving drinks but no meals. Whitehead was immediately put to work as both a lingual and cultural interpreter and spent as much time teaching the British officers why the Poles would want to do something different as he did educating the Poles to the RAF way of doing things. Eventually the Polish ways won and most of the English staff moved to other units leaving the squadron almost entirely staffed by Poles. A very popular officer at this time was F.F.E. Yeo-Thomas who was engaged as the squadron's Intelligence Officer. He and Whitehead found they had a lot in common both being from ex-patriot families and from a similar class; business and educational background and they became firm lifetime friends.

Yeo-Thomas pursued his ambition to take the fight to the Germans on French soil by applying and being accepted to RF section of SOE. Initially he was employed as a liaison officer for the BCRA but the following year Whitehead bumped into Yeo-Thomas in London, as his squadron had been re-deployed to the Polish mother station at Northolt. This meeting sparked a desire in Whitehead to do something more proactive and at the beginning of 1943 he applied to be posted to the Polish section of SOE. He subsequently had an interview in Whitehall with the head of the Polish section Colonel Perkins but at that time there were no vacancies (the actual reason was that unknown to George his brother Alfred had already been accepted into the Polish section and it was not possible to employ him likewise). Disappointed he again saw Yeo-Thomas who was just back from his second mission and had been to see the Prime Minister who had authorised the expansion of help for the French resistance and Whitehead was recruited to RF section and after training assigned to Citronelle as the administration officer.

CAPITAINE CHAVANE

Jacques Chavane was born on 3rd January 1914 Lunéville, Meurthe-et-Moselle in the Lorraine region of France. He was called to military service on 1st October 1935 and entered to the Chasseurs d'Afrique, a light cavalry corps. He was promoted to sous-lieutenant in 1936 and posted to Strasbourg. In 1937 he was de-mobilised and returned home but was recalled on 27th August 1939 and on 25th April 1940 promoted to full lieutenant. Following the fall of France and the armistice he was again de-mobilised where he made himself available to the General commanding the 19th military district and was assigned to the 5th Regiment of Chasseurs d'Afrique in May 1941. He was again demobilised in Tunisia on 1st January 1942 but was recalled to the 2nd Regiment of Cuirassiers. He joined the BCRA in Algiers on 24th November 1943 and travelled immediately to Britain where he received training including Parachute at Ringway.

He was assigned the field name 'Point', promoted temporary captain on 1st June 1944 and joined the Citronelle team as intelligence officer. The choice of the name Point was unfortunate as it was also the nickname of the Ardennes resistance leader Captain Fournier, wanted by the Gestapo. French records state he was also appointed as second in command of Citronelle which is rather odd due to his last minute appointment to the team and his role as intelligence officer was to keep him away from the mission forming networks and gathering information.

LIEUTENANT LUCIEN

Lucien Charles Goetghebeur was born on 1st August 1923 in Créteil, south east of Paris. After leaving school he worked as an apprentice goldsmith in Paris and was still working in this capacity when the Second World War started. At the end of 1942 he made the decision to leave France to join the Free French Forces in London. He escaped France into Spain on 26th January 1943 but was arrested by the Spanish police and interned in Pamplona until 25th February. He managed to leave Spain for Portugal and at Setúbal near Lisbon he boarded a ship bound for Morocco on 14th May.

In Morocco he joined the Free French Army and was assigned to the 4th Bataillon d'infanterie de l'Air (French Special Forces) on

July 13th and then travelled by aeroplane to London on 20th September where he joined the BCRA. He volunteered for a mission to return to France and after paramilitary and parachute training he was assigned to Mission Citronelle in the rank of sous-lieutenant as a sabotage instructor with the field name Echardonnette. (An échardonnette is a sickle for cutting thistles).

It can be noted here that all the above members of the Mission Citronelle have a defined role except Desmond and there are a number of possible explanations for this based on a combination of factors. Firstly Desmond was originally assigned to another mission but became available when it was discovered that Gestapo infiltration had compromised this group. There were many staff officers in SOE who were anxious to get into action and the D-Day planners needed everyone they could get. Desmond although experienced within SOE and senior in rank by virtue of time than Capitaine Chavane, lacked operational experience in the field and needed both operational and command experience. It was expected that Citronelle would become too large for one SOE team and it was intended to split when this time came. Desmond would have been well placed to command a splinter group. Another factor was, after the planning stages of Citronelle and between the insertion dates of Citronelle one and two, Desmond was selected to attend a training course in propaganda. The region of the Ardennes was difficult to assess in advance and the need for propaganda to undermine the German forces and encourage French men and women to support the Allied cause was undoubtedly a requirement and no doubt seen as an asset by Commandant Bollardière who was in the field.

The target area for Citronelle was the Ardennes, on the north eastern border of France and Belgium, the northern part of this region is mainly mountainous and forested and the Southern mainly agricultural. It was unique in that when the German forces invaded France the population was compulsorily evacuated but when they were allowed to return to their homes, the Germans had established a firm control and the Todt organisation had drafted in workers from other areas. No one knew who to trust and there were many collaborators willing to help the Germans for better rations, money or treatment. During 1944 the Gestapo had huge success against the French resistance and it was not clearly established if there was an organised resistance movement in the area. Available intelligence reports stated that there were approximately 800 resistants in the area but there were no suitable landing zones established. As planning continued it became apparent that these intelligence reports were inaccurate and that the area had been neglected by the resistance hierarchy and that there were in fact no armed resistants but in the region of 60 potential dropping sites. This lack of organised resistance was the reason for the need for an Inter-Allied Mission as opposed to a Jedburgh team. Citronelle, meaning Lemongrass, a fragrant herb, was an example of how several Inter-Allied Missions were so named. In total 26 Inter-allied missions were sent to France in support of D-Day or the battle for France between April and September 1944.

THE PLAN

The Operational Instructions for Mission Citronelle are dated March 11th 1944 and start with a number of points of information:

- It mentions that there are Maquis groups in the Ardennes but little is known of their strengths and organisation.
- The groups were headed by 'Jerome' the Chef National du Maquis. Jerome is aware of the mission and team members had discussed it with him thus Jerome was obviously involved in the planning stages.
- The danger of over centralisation of the resistance is stressed, as is the need to organise action to coincide with the immediate needs of the Allied High Command.
- There is also a stark warning at this stage about the Belgian Troupes Secretes who had been involved across the border with the French Maquis, but there was serious doubt about the security of this group. The members of the mission were not to have any dealings with them or any other Belgian resistance network. The problem in Belgium was the Rexist movement, who were a collaborative Fascist organisation in full support of Hitler.

The intention was stated that:

- The mission was to proceed into the field during the March intermoon or the April moon.
- To make contact with persons nominated by Jerome who would then make contact with Chiefs of the Ardennes Resistance.
- To represent the views of the Allied High Command to the military chiefs of the Ardennes.
- To extend the mission at a later date, if deemed appropriate, to the Vosges and Argonne Departments. The order of the mission was to take effect when all members of the mission were in the field.

The method was firstly for the Commander Prisme, Triedre and Senegalais to parachute into France with the sole responsibility of finding an appropriate landing zone for the rest of the mission to join them. At this planning stage the members of the mission were Commander Bollardière (Prisme), Captain Hubble (Bissectrice), Lieutenant Layton (Triedre), the wireless operator Lieutenant Brault (Senegalais) and Flight Lieutenant Whitehead the admin officer. It was later in the field that the need for an intelligence officer and sabotage instructors was determined and the additions made.

A reception committee was organised for the first drop and in the event of this not being successful a safe house address was given as a meeting place. A cover story and false papers were devised for all the members of the mission. In the table at the start of Part VI, it can be seen that the false names were all using the real first name of the respective agent except for Desmond. The simple explanation for this is that Desmond is not a French name, whereas all the other names are either French or have a French equivalent. The best liars tell as much of the truth as possible and in a stressful situation it is easier to remember truths without giving signs of trying to remember a lie, such as eye movement. The other name shown in the table is the name which each member was to be known to the Maquis, in Desmond's case Capitaine Alain. In the event of a Maquis member falling into the hands of the Gestapo they had no knowledge which would make any identity papers useless.

From an administration point it was re-iterated that the purpose of the mission was to ensure that the Chiefs of Departments were to make a more effective organisation of the various Maquis groups, for the purpose of ensuring their activities were in accordance of the wishes of the Allied High Command for the support of the D-Day landings. It also states that a few small units were to be constituted, comparable to the military formations introduced into the country by parachute and hidden until needed following the invasion, this alludes to the three man Jedburgh teams.

Firm instructions were given that the mission would not in any sense command the Maquis groups and the limitations were to:

1. Report to London on the locations of camps, strength in numbers and armaments, recommendations of the type and numbers of armaments needed by the groups. Specific mention is made of Bren and Sten guns.
2. To create a liaison between the Military Chiefs and London.
3. Assistance and advice to the Military Chiefs in matters of security, organisation, day to day sabotage and D-Day plans.
4. Reconnoitring and reporting to London of suitable drop zones for parachuting agents and supplies plus any potential places for landing operations (Lysander/ Hudson). One or more of the former sites which could be readily defended against armed assault for 24 – 48 hours and to which material and uniformed troops could be delivered on or about D-Day. The dimensions of such grounds to be 3-4 Km sq. thereby permitting parachute descent from high altitude.
5. The administration officer was responsible for all the record keeping of the mission and their safekeeping and destruction if necessary. He was also responsible for the stores of the mission and their distribution.

6. The wireless operator was responsible for all messages sent and received and work under the mission in all aspects except technical where he was to use his own discretion.
7. If, once in the field, the mission reports the need for sabotage instructors or further W/T operator they will be sent.

The issue of recruitment to the Maquis was dealt with and the statement made that quality rather than quantity was desired. The fact that the dispensing of men already enrolled, who were not of the quality required, would be very difficult and was acknowledged but stress was placed on the importance of maintaining a rigorous control over all who apply to join.

Author's note (*In the forests and mountains of France there were many young men who were displaced from their homes to avoid the compulsory conscription to work for the German war effort. The French word for these men is* 'réfractaires' *and the closest English translation is 'deserter'. The English word denotes a sense of negativity which these loyal Frenchmen do not deserve, as they chose to live without family, rations and legality in favour of collaboration with the Nazi and Vichy regimes; I choose to continue using the word* réfractaire *which denotes a sense of honour).*

The mission was to be financed with large sums of French Francs taken by the mission members, the three main members, Bollardière, Layton and Desmond were each to take 1,500,000 Francs, the administration officer was to be financed out of Desmond's money but also had 50,000 Francs for operational expenses. The W/T operator was also allocated 50,000 Francs.

This part of the planning stage is also the first clue in what became known in the locality as the 'Citronelle Treasure'. Since the end of the war a local fable talks of a great treasure buried in the forest by the mission, those in officialdom have always denied that such a treasure ever existed and that the mission was funded by a local bank in Revin, the nearest large town. Further documents, including French resistance records, show that large quantities of French Francs were taken to the Ardennes and the truth has been suppressed for very good financial reasons. During the planning of the invasion of Europe large quantities of French Franc bank notes were made available to pay for the armies as they went in respect of local reparations and for payment of bills incurred. General de Gaulle, whose intentions for France included post war planning, saw this as potentially disastrous for the French economy and fought against the plan. The worth of a currency is very much based on the trust placed in it and Hitler had authorised a plan to undermine the British economy by having huge quantities of British £5 notes forged and then introduced to the British economy via air drops. This would have broken the British economy and forced Britain to sue for peace. It would certainly have been in the interests of the post war French establishment to deny that such a treasure ever existed to maintain confidence in the economy.

The issue of stores, including arms, is noted and gives an indication of the situation with regards to equipment at the time. A massive amount of stores and arms was required in support of the Invasion and what was occurring in the Ardennes was also happening all over France, the basic intent being to tie up as many enemy troops as possible to give the landings the best possible chance of success. While it was noted that the immediate distribution of arms to the Maquis groups was desirable, it was also stated that the support both in arms and finance to these groups should be confined to those elements which could be used directly against the enemy forces.

> *"Our assistance, both in materials and finance, must be limited to the support of those elements which we can use directly against the enemy. We are more than willing to send essential materials to and to spend more money upon feeding, disciplined and active men who can be relied upon to accept orders and to carry them out"*. (National Archives file HS 6/358).

Sabotage targets are identified in the plan but the initial wording shows that there was little information to direct specific targets in advance. It also reflects that there was no advanced knowledge of any existing resistance groups in the area as there is contingency planning for training of any groups formed and then targets could be identified dependent on the experience and competence of the individuals recruited. Specifically mentioned as targets in general terms are those targets thought to cause maximum degree of dispersal of German occupying troops, disrupting and destroying the Luftwaffe, a priority list is given:

1. Disruption and destruction of the G.A.F. (Luftwaffe), particularly fighter aircraft, fighter repair shops, factories producing aircraft bodies and machinery, petrol and oil dumps and air force H.Q.
2. Petrol and oil dumps.
3. Enemy military communications.

Guerrilla activities were similarly listed but noted that it was the team's responsibility to impress on the military chiefs of the departments that on or after D-Day it is the organisation of such activities that was to be their most important duty:

1. Dislocation of road communications and telecommunications.
2. Disruption and harassing of enemy H.Q.
3. Destruction of fuel dumps.
4. Attacks on the G.A.F., particularly fighter aircraft and fighter aircraft repair workshops.
5. Destruction of ammunition dumps.

The instruction was for the identification of targets falling into these categories, reporting them back for instruction as to whether they should be automatically attacked or to await instruction for a specific attack order. The mention of the Luftwaffe shows the importance placed on dominance of the air for the success of the invasion which was the main reason Hitler postponed his plans for the invasion of Britain, the Luftwaffe's failure to destroy the RAF.

One other specific instruction given was for the organisation, when called upon to foment and support uprisings by the civilian population and also to encourage strikes and lockouts. This would clearly have fallen within the remit of Desmond's training at STS 39 the Hackett School for subversive propaganda.

The plan draws conclusions which deal with the issue of limitations of delivery of stores due to the topographical and meteorological conditions of the area. Communications for these deliveries were the use of Eureka for which Desmond had received the necessary training at STS 40.

One other point to mention about the objectives of Citronelle, but not mentioned at this stage in the plans, was the River Meuse running through the region formed a massive natural barrier to form a defensive line behind. Citronelle's duty was to help prevent the German forces establishing a defensive position in the event of the invasion and subsequent battle for France being successful.

THE MISSION

At 9.30 p.m. on April 11th 1944 an aircraft took off from an airfield in the South of England. On board were the first three elements of Mission Citronelle, Commandant Bollardière, Lieutenant Layton and Lieutenant Brault. Over the coast of France the flight was disturbed by light Flak fire from anti-aircraft gun emplacements and over the drop zone, near Mourmelon le Grand in the Champagne-Ardennes region, the 'Joe hole' was opened and the instruction given by the dispatcher, 'Action stations'. Commandant Bollardière, as leader was first and grabbing the sides of the hole allowed his legs to dangle into space. His two companions formed up behind him ready for their turn. The order for number one to go is given and he is followed very closely by Layton and then by Brault. The aeroplane turns to go home as the silk parachutes blossom open. The three men drift gradually down towards the lights of the reception committee; Layton later reported that he lost sight of the lights on the way down and as soon as he landed he changed his jump boots, buried his chute and waited for the reception committee to find him. After 20 minutes he heard French voices and he was joined by four women and two men who told him he had missed the drop zone by a mile and was actually inside the perimeter of a German training camp. The group then searched for the other team members who had also landed astray by about one mile. After finding the packages which had been dropped with the agents, a messenger was despatched to Paris to obtain the contact details of the Maquis leaders in the Ardennes. The team were met with the usual hospitality greeting of French people from this area, two bottles of Champagne, which after consuming, the group travelled in a gasogene powered lorry to a local farm called, “Ferme de L’Esperance”, where they spent the day in hiding. At one point German soldiers arrived at the farm but it was to buy eggs and a tense moment ended with great relief. Later in the evening the agents were taken to a safe house in Mourmelon where they stayed for a week with a garage owner. Finally four Free French resistants arrived, Colonel Gilbert Hirsch-Ollendorf, code name Planète, the head of the Délégué Militaire Régional (DMR) for region C (includes Ardennes), Commandant Aubusson Planète’s Chief of Staff and two messenger-body guards. Planète confirmed that there was no organised resistance in the Ardennes and made arrangements for the agents to be transported to the Ardennes to Renwez a small community between Rocroi and Charleville where they were introduced to the Chief of the local Gendarmerie, Brigadier Pierrard. On the way, to what was thought to be a safe hiding place, an empty house hidden in the woods near a swamp, it was discovered that the Germans had recently searched this house several times looking for réfractaires and were instead taken to a hut on the other side of the swamp. Safely ensconced here Sénégalais set up the radio and the first messages of Mission Citronelle were sent to London to update with regards to the situation as it existed.

The sending of messages via radio from enemy occupied territory was a hazardous business and Lieutenant Brault was well qualified to testify to this fact having been previously engaged in the field and in fact captured as a result of radio direction finding equipment. The Germans had developed an efficient system of radio detection which involved a minimum of two vans with radio receivers on board. The listener would turn the roof antenna until the strongest signal was found and then take a compass bearing from their position to the source of the signal. Two vehicles, in different locations both reporting a direction, made it easy to locate the radio by triangulating the signals on a map.

Desmond and George Whitehead had been waiting impatiently for news of the forward party and when finally messages started to come in they made themselves busy getting together all the materials and equipment requested and planning the next stages of the mission.

The original plan made it clear that the forward party's only responsibility at this stage was to make contact and locate a suitable landing ground for use to bring the rest of the mission into the field. There is no revision in the paperwork but the plan was obviously changed as additions were made to the personnel and the second half of the mission was delayed until D-Day.

In their hut the forward party had sufficient 24 hour rations for three days and decided to stretch them as far as they could. After two days a meeting was arranged with the French Forces of the Interior (FFI) leader of the area André Fournier, also known as Commandant Point, who took them in his panel van to another safe location, a dug out underground shelter below a 900 ft. cliff, near Laifour, overlooking a large loop in the Meuse river. The team stayed here for four weeks and their only visitors were two poachers, but Fournier arranged for food to be brought to them until air drops could be organised and they could then fend for themselves. Apart from the radio equipment all the team had at this stage was six Sten guns and ammunition, side arms and 20 Mills bombs.

From the start and throughout the mission there was suspicion shown about the purpose of Citronelle from resistance leaders, as unbeknown to the team, another mission was active in the area called Plan Paul. Plan Paul had almost the same terms and objectives as Citronelle and understandably the resistance leaders were cautious and relationships remained cordial, though not all agreements made at meetings were carried out. Bollardière was only interested in getting his mission active and requested that the resistance leaders send him some réfractaires to be trained and form the nucleus of a Maquis. Aubusson the Chief of staff agreed to this request and directed that Fournier take care of recruiting men of the right calibre and getting payment to their families, setting up food stocks at various locations in the forest, passing intelligence about German forces and acting as liaison agent for the group. He also named the Maquis group Prisme, the code-name for Bollardière.

On 25th April 1944 a message was sent to London with a request for sufficient arms and equipment to supply 180 men in the field. They received a reply via the BBC on 5th May, '*The hare is bolting*', which informed the team that the drop was to be made to a field code named Bohémien. That night at about 10 p.m. the team left their dugout and moved to the area known as Hauts-Buttes which is a high plateau area, forested and very remote. The Manise Forest and river is part of this terrain. At the Bohémien field they met the nominated reception committee led by a local farmer M. Machaud, Whilst the team maintained security the reception committee formed up to provide lights, the local electricity line had been cut especially for the occasion and the aeroplane passed overhead twice at about 2.30 a.m. By this time it was freezing cold as this area; even in May is very unforgiving. The drop was made on the third circle over the field and 15 containers and four packages were collected and hidden at this location.

The following night the drops were collected and taken to a pre-prepared cache which was where they intended to form a camp for the Maquis. At the break of dawn the containers and packages were opened to the huge disappointment of those present. There was little of what had been ordered and what was correct was not in sufficient numbers for the purpose. They had ordered 180 sleeping bags, rucksacks and musettes plus buckets and camping equipment to survive in the wild, there were however, lamps without batteries, picks and shovels, a very small amount of corned beef and sufficient arms for only 60 men. The weather was so bad that it was raining and freezing every night and what had been sent was wholly inadequate for the objectives of the mission. The equipment was divided into five groups of ten, the first two groups were well armed and the next three groups had to be juggled to make ends meet. They were assisted by three men who were their first recruits to the Maquis. The following morning the first tragedy of the mission occurred, at 4 am one of the local resistants, M. Thomérée, fell from his bicycle and died without regaining consciousness. The assistance of local officials had to be sought to falsify official reports in order to hide the true nature of the incident.

Fournier proved to be less than co-operative. The team believed he had grand ambitions for his own private army and that by assisting the mission he would reduce his power in the Ardennes. Initially he sent approximately 30 men none of whom met the high standard required for the job. Two of the men were blind in one eye; one was lame and over a dozen were aged in excess of forty five. They were described by Layton as, "the trash of all his (Fournier's) sections". Strong words indeed for a man who had a strong affinity for the French which remained with him until his death! The team were very disappointed in the support they had received from London and from Fournier but decided that they had no choice but to make the best of what they had and commenced to train the men in the handling of the arms that they had received.

At about this time Desmond attended and passed the subversive propaganda course at Hackett School and the services of a local priest were sought to look after the spiritual needs of the men in the forest, Father Marie-Antoine de Willerzie eagerly accepts the role.

On or around the 25th May the Maquis Prisme moved location to a camp on the south side of a hill but north of the Manise River in the Manise Forest. A few of the recruits had become disillusioned with camp life and had returned home and Bollardière had made the decision to move for security reasons. They had recovered several parachutes from the first air drop and due to the lack of supplies they were forced to use these in lieu of tents. The better equipped men camped in the forest, whilst local farmers, who were members of the resistance, made provision on the farms for the rest of the men. These farmers also provided food as Fournier had not honoured his commitment to set up food stores. A group of ladies of the area fabricated a French tricolour flag with the Cross of Lorraine on it and this was proudly flown over the camp and life was not considered too bad.

Among these farmers were M. Fontaine and his family, wife Mme Marguerite, sons Louis-Georges and Gaston and daughter Mlle Georgette. The family farm was very close to the Belgian border and within site of the border guards, many of whom both French and Belgian were in the resistance. At the beginning of the war Marguerite Fontaine had started to write a diary of events and M. Fontaine had made a hole in a beam in the cowshed for her to hide her notes. This is the Journal de Marguerite Fontaine, a contemporaneous account of events and now seen as an extremely important historical document of the period; after the war the papers were published. The Fontaine family were typical of people from the area, hard-working, unassuming and fervently patriotic. The fall of France and the betrayal of the Vichy Government was a great shock and shame and they were determined to do something to right the wrongs. They were constantly in danger of betrayal by collaborators or discovery by the Germans and frequentlyharassed in the search for réfractaires or resistants. On one occasion German forces attended the farm to search it and British military kit was hanging up in the dining room, if this had been found the family would have at least been sent to a prison camp such as Compiegne or worse, possibly shot out of hand. While M. Fontaine kept the soldiers talking, his daughter Georgette, who was 18 at the time, removed the items from the room by climbing out of a window and burying them in the animal manure in the barn. This sort of bravery is what makes the people of this area special and extremely proud of their part in this history. The Fontaine Farm was visited by Bollardière looking for a new drop site. He was accompanied by Captain Levard who introduces his companion to Mme Fontaine:

"Madam, I am honoured to introduce to you a Commander of Free France".

Mme Fontaine's reaction tells of the emotion of the moment and of the frustration of the years of oppression and waiting for this day. "*Free France….Free Zone…I can't quite grasp it, so great is my emotion. It is as if I am rooted to the spot, finally I almost shout, "One of De Gaulle's men" tears come to my eyes, "sir we owe you everything, you are our hope.*"

Her daughter Georgette is as moved as her mother and it takes a while to get their emotions under control. They show the officers a large field near to the farm and Bollardière chooses it for the drop zone for men and names it Astrologie, the tree line along one side of this field is the Belgian border.

Astrologie was used for the first time on Whit Sunday 28th May; nearly everyone from the Haut-Buttes area is involved. Mme Fontaine records in her diary:

"*It is Whit Sunday. A joyful Odette Machaux arrived bringing the great news. We busy ourselves for a reception which we hope will be worthy of French tradition. In the parachute group there will be allied officers and they must retain a very good impression of their arrival in France. I have been keeping some stocks back with them in mind which we have been guarding jealously. We are helped by our neighbour and god-daughter, the elder daughter of M. Machaux, she has two children.*"

The Fontaine household is then busy all day making preparations for the parachute drop, food, champagne, beds made and even water is boiled in the event of first aid being required. Near to the time the area becomes filled with resistants, officers and customs officials who are all going to help with the reception committee. An armed guard is placed around the few houses nearby and Mme Fontaine is told to ensure all light is blocked out from her windows and when she tries to come outside she is ordered at gunpoint back into the house. A resistant who knows her corrects this situation and the household are allowed outside to watch the proceedings. The women choose to stay in the kitchen ensuring no light is shown and keeping the cooking pots and water ready for the arrival of the men, the resistant with the machine gun has frightened them.

In the Astrologie field Georges Fontaine holds a red recognition lamp and Victor Layton has been in communication with the aircraft on his S-Phone. At midnight a thunderous roar is heard as numerous aeroplanes fly directly over the farm, the house shudders with the noise, the planes have dropped a total of 45 containers and 40 packages. Shortly after the drop the aircraft fly off and a man appears at the door of the Fontaine Farm and announces that there were no men, but containers are all over the fields and they need poles to remove them to the cache prepared for the occasion in a thicket in one of the Farm's meadows. Some of the containers weigh 200 kg and require four men to carry them to the cache. One of the container parachutes had failed to open and the container had entered the ground, burst open and there were broken rifles scattered in the field. All of these containers parachutes and debris had to be cleared and hidden before the German forces at Croix-Saille had a chance to investigate. The field is cleared and as everyone goes home three more containers are found in gardens and these are also hidden. The Maquis have to hide locally and food is taken to them in the woods, everyone is disappointed that the drop did not have parachutists as they know that the time for their liberation is near and the first sign that this great event is about to happen is the arrival of these officers.

Amongst the arms delivered in this drop were Bazookas, 90 carbines, Mills and Gamon bombs, Sten and Bren guns and several hundred pounds of high explosive. There were more sleeping bags and clothing but insufficient for the expectations of the mission. Victor Layton believed that the containers had not been packed properly and the details of the messages they had sent requesting supplies had not been read properly.

DESMOND'S ARRIVAL

On the 5th June the BBC transmitted the following message, "*Le roi Jean est sage; cinq amis viendront ce soir visiter le roi Jean*". (King John is wise; five friends will visit King John this evening). This was the message that told the men in the field that Desmond and Citronelle 2 were on the way.

During the day of the 5th Desmond and the others were taken to a safe house near Harrington airfield, station 179, near Kettering, Northamptonshire the home of 36th Special Duty Bomber Squadron. The normal procedure on these occasions was to ensure that the agents were prepared for insertion into enemy territory in that they were not carrying or wearing anything which would compromise their cover story of who they were and what their business was. To this end SOE had taken such steps as hiring French seamstresses, who would be able to make clothing in current French styles, collating intelligence about what was difficult to obtain etc. It was essential that agents blended in to the area where they were to operate not just from a language point of view but to be aware of what to ask for in cafes, hotels and bars. An agent could be betrayed by having the wrong cigarettes in his pocket or a type of shoes which were difficult to obtain, they could not be too careful as the German and Vichy forces were adept at picking out those who did not appear to belong. On this occasion it appears these rules were relaxed as Desmond was allowed to take his favourite pipe and a travelling chess set which had been a present from his mother. He was also in possession of letters, which although it is not certain of the content, were likely to be compromising. The difference on this occasion may be that this half of the team was travelling with uniform to identify them as allied combatants as well as civilian clothes.

Hubble's Chess set (Author's picture)

Jump suits and parachute packs were checked and then they boarded their flight to France, B-42-63980 Playmate a USAF special duty flight under the command of Ernest S. Holzworth, for this mission, using the call sign of B for Bertie. The packages and containers which accompanied the mission had been loaded to the bomb bays of the aircraft by ground crew in the day. The only member of the eight member crew that the mission members had contact with was the despatcher H.E. Siewart whose job was to keep nerves at bay with small talk and supply warm drinks from flasks.

The mission was first notified the previous evening at about 5 p.m. to the station's Intelligence officer, who then spent the evening plotting the various missions onto a map. All missions are marked separately and the SOE missions were distinctly marked. The following morning the squadron commanders held a meeting to determine which crews would be used for which mission. It is normal practice that if there is a disagreement the flip of a coin determines the matter. At midday each navigator is given the target and determines a flight plan, many factors come to play including the likelihood of flak on the route and over the target; they also have a weather report to assist them. Following this each crew is individually briefed by the intelligence officer and a final briefing of all crews is held at 4.30 p.m. Individual briefings are held as necessary the radio operator will be briefed as to the recognition signals and in the case of Citronelle 2 the recognition is 'R' for Robert both flashed by torchlight from the ground and transmitted via Rebecca. Between these fixed appointments the crew will give the aircraft an inspection and a half hour test flight is conducted. Apart from the packages and parcels which have been loaded onto Playmate, leaflets to be dropped on the way home were also put on board, these leaflets were called 'Nickels' and packed in bundles of 4,000 and on this night Playmate carried 10 bundles of propaganda leaflets to be dropped after Citronelle 2, near to Brussels. These leaflets were prepared by the Psychological Warfare Division of SHAEF and were either the Eisenhower Proclamation or a message to Belgian railway workers. They were designed as a forewarning for the civilian population of areas to be targeted by bombing campaigns in the support of the D-Day landings and had been insisted on by the French (probably de Gaulle) via Prime Minister Churchill who was adamant that *'in post war Europe France must be our friend'*.

During the evening Desmond and the other 'Joes' were delivered to the airfield by SOE escorting officers where they were received by the armaments officer. Playmate took off at 23.25 hrs and set course for France, in total 11 aircraft took off that night, one craft failed to return and was marked 'MIA'. They passed over the coast of England over Orford Ness in Suffolk at midnight at a height of 6,600 ft. The flight was uneventful, crossing into enemy occupied Europe at Tholen in Holland and then through Belgium to the Ardennes. On reaching the drop zone at 01.15 the despatcher told the agents to prepare to jump. They hooked their parachute lines to the overhead cable and crouched in line at the Joe hole, first man's legs dangling through the hole. This hole in the floor of the B42 was the belly machine gun turret removed and replaced with a trap door. Over the target at 550 ft. the green light was given and the despatcher gave the signal to go, each man in turn dropped through the hole and the static lines opened the parachute packs, at this height the descent would only have taken between 15-30 seconds depending on conditions. In turn each chute billowed into a huge mushroom and slowed the descent of the agent. The cold Ardennes night hit them in the face as they slowly descended to the waiting signal lights and the reception committee below.

It was a huge relief to be safely down on the ground but not the end of their stress as they were now in enemy controlled territory and faced a ruthless and brutal foe, whose only concern was to capture and kill as many of their enemies to further their standing in the eyes of their evil Fuhrer. When the last of the agents had jumped the despatcher informed the pilot, who then turned to make a second run to drop the parcels and packages; in total the aircraft was over the target area for 16 minutes. Following the drop the crew of Playmate turned away and headed for St Nicholas near Brussels where they dropped their bundles of leaflets and then headed back to Harrington for de-briefing by the intelligence officer, a good breakfast and then bed.

Astrologie the far tree line is the French/Belgian border (Author's Photo)

LA FERME FONTAINE (THE FONTAINE FARM)

Under the command of Bollardière, a reception committee had been formed and reinforced with 15 men from the border control guards. At the Fontaine farm similar arrangements as previous are in place to receive Desmond and the others. Mme Fontaine requests that security guards are kept away from the house to avoid another incident. She and the other women prepare food, wine, beds and hot water; it is most important for them all to make a favourable impression on the allied officers. Victor Layton again takes up position in the field and takes charge of the S-Phone, but as the plane approaches he experiences difficulty in making contact as the batteries are not good. The parachute drops, both men and equipment are successful and the latter was hidden under tree branches and other litter in the middle of Astrologie.

The first people to go to the Fontaine farm were Captain Jacques Chavane and Lieutenant Lucien Goetghebeur escorted by Captain Levard who introduces them: "*Two Frenchmen Captain Jacques and Lieutenant Lucien.*"

All embrace in a tremendous moment of emotion, the visitors are asked what they would like to drink the reply from Captain Jacques is of course, "*For me, French wine*".

They remove their jump suits and headgear and show that they wear the khaki uniform and insignia of the Free French Forces and empty their pockets of revolvers and grenades, the table is covered in hardware. Lieutenant Goetghebeur had fallen into a swamp and has to change his socks. They are pressed as to when the invasion will occur but decide to be evasive and will only say it is some months away. They leave and then Victor Layton comes to the farm with three more uniformed officers, Desmond and the rest of Citronelle 2.

Gérard Racine introduces himself and exclaims, "*Frenchwomen, I feel closer to my mother and sister!*" He introduces Desmond and George who shake hands with everyone and make polite, kind comments in heavily accented French. They are shortly joined by Commandant Bollardière who has with him two allied aviators, one American and one Canadian who have been with the Maquis for a few days.

Desmond has brought mail from London and the Commander reads this under the light of an oil lamp. He is pleased by what he reads and no doubt this was the announcement that D-Day had arrived.

Dining Room, Fontaine Farmhouse. (Author's photo)

There is little time but the politics of the situation demand that time is taken for a celebratory reception. The men are taken through to the dining room where the table has been covered with a cloth of white parachute material. In the centre is the proud slogan continually repeated by the BBC '*Honour and homeland*'. The four corners of the table cloth have been embroidered with the American, Belgian, French and English flags and the mantelpiece has a spray of Lilly-of-the-valley which permeates a delightful aroma around the room. The room is lit by a centrally hung acetylene lamp giving the setting a certain sparkle. Desmond and the other visitors are astonished and delighted by the scene and soon 11 men are seated around the table, uniforms mingle with the threadbare jackets and clothing of the Maquis. A simple meal and wine is shared and compliments and praise are heaped upon the hosts. Mme Fontaine proudly records that once again the cuisine and wine of France are praised. Mlle Georgette Fontaine pours wine and serves food to the guests.

The party is joined by the reception committee who have hidden the containers. M. Fontaine has recovered a small parachute which has delivered a cage holding four pigeons, to be released to report to London that the mission had arrived in the event of the radio malfunctioning. It is not recorded what happened to all the pigeons, two were taken back to camp, another released to return to London, perhaps the other were released perhaps not, after all in times such as these food was not wasted.

When the meal is finished Champagne is opened and Victor Layton tells the hosts how much the English officers are moved by the welcome and announces that Desmond would like to give a toast, he speaks in English and afterwards Layton translates. Mme Fontaine records:

"*His great height dominates the group. We cannot understand his words but we can feel the sentiments they express. Indeed the translation informs us that the English are profoundly touched by the efficiency of the help with which the Free French Forces of General de Gaulle and of the resistance within France have given in the common struggle for the freedom of peoples.*

'This union', says the Captain, is making unshakable links of friendship since they are sealed in mutual danger.

Although Lieutenant Layton has finished talking he remains on his feet; in this moment of silence he says these words, Dear friends, I have the privilege of telling you that we have gone onto the third level of alert. Therefore the invasion is imminent.'

Looking at his watch he says, 'At this moment it has probably already happened'."

It is an indicator of the high regard in which Desmond was held by Commandant Bollardière that he chose to allow an Englishman to deliver this incredibly important piece of news to the local people and also to his sense of politics. The English are not always well regarded in France and the Ardennes is no exception. To allow this news to be delivered in this fashion could only have enhanced the feeling of solidarity. There is a stunned silence broken only by one man's words of thanks.

Shortly afterwards the mission and Maquis have to leave as dawn is imminent; they are guided to the camp along small infrequently used pathways by Gaston Fontaine. Shortly after all the men had left the open fields, a Luftwaffe fighter plane flew low over the area at 100 ft. The aeroplane was conducting a reconnaissance mission because of night time activity, which even in such a remote place could not go unnoticed due to the noise of the low level bombers.

The mission lay low for three days before returning to recover the hidden equipment. Again there were deficiencies in what had been delivered but not as serious as the first drops.

THE CAMP

Desmond set about making a complete inventory of what had been delivered and what was needed as there were serious deficiencies. The weather for June 1944 was bad and with the conditions in this remote mountainous area, living in the forest required good camping and personal equipment. It was also desired to put all recruits into some form of uniform for their protection in the event of capture and to instil a sense of unity and military

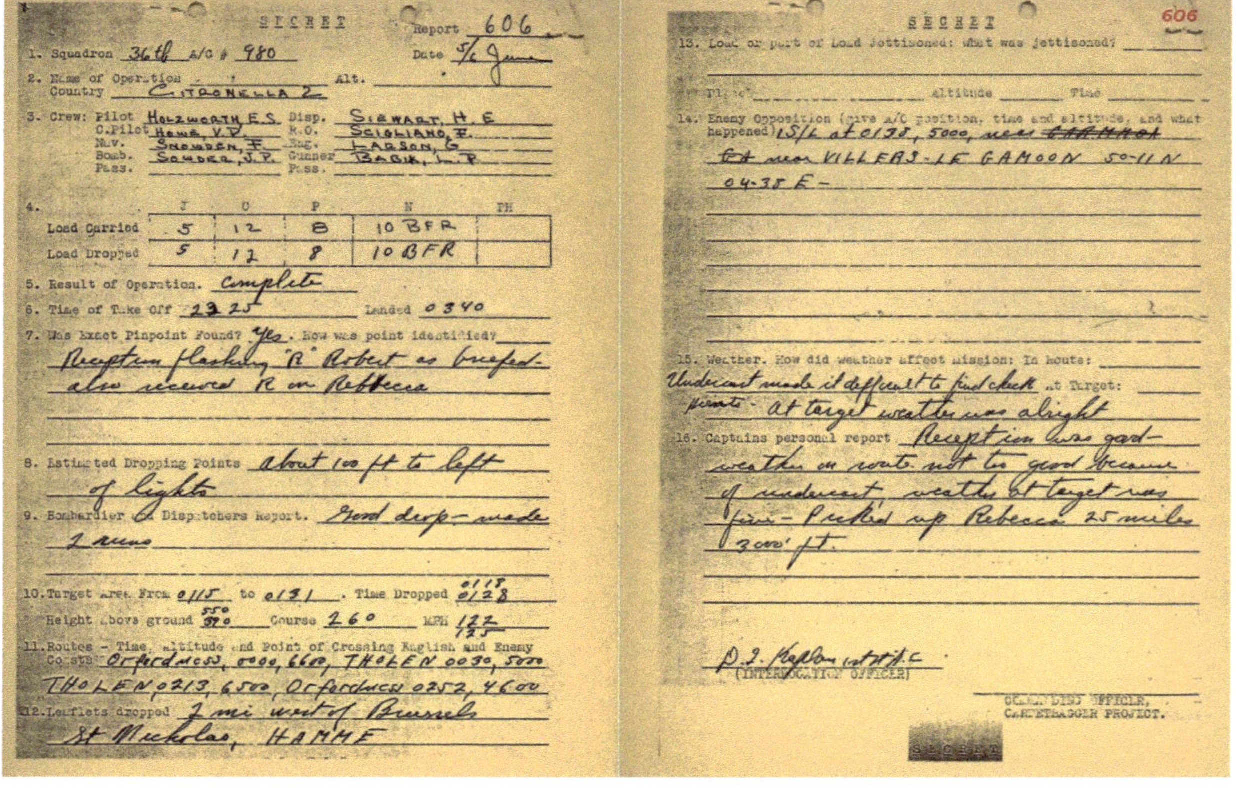
SECRET

Report 606

1. Squadron 36th A/C # 980 Date 5/6 June

2. Name of Operation
Country CITRONELLA 2 Alt.

3. Crew: Pilot HOLZWORTH, E.S. Disp. STEWART, H. E.
C.Pilot HOWE, V.P. R.O. SCIGLIANO, F.
Nav. SNOWDEN, F. Eng. LARSON, G.
Bomb. SANDER, J.P. Gunner BABIK, L.P.
Pass. Pass.

4.

	J	C	P	N	PH
Load Carried	5	12	8	10 BFR	
Load Dropped	5	12	8	10 BFR	

5. Result of Operation. complete

6. Time of Take Off 23 25 Landed 0340

7. Was Exact Pinpoint Found? Yes. How was point identified? Reception flashing "R" Robert as briefed – also received R on Rebecca

8. Estimated Dropping Points about 100 ft to left of lights

9. Bombardier or Dispatchers Report. Good drop – made 2 runs

10. Target Area From 0115 to 0131. Time Dropped 0118 0128
Height above ground 550 590 Course 260 MPH 122 125

11. Routes – Time, altitude and Point of Crossing English and Enemy Coasts Orfordness, 0000, 6600, THOLEN 0030, 5000 THOLEN 0213, 6500, Orfordness 0252, 4600

12. Leaflets dropped 2 mi west of Brussels St Nickolas, HAMME

SECRET

606

13. Load or part of Load Jettisoned: What was jettisoned?
Place Altitude Time

14. Enemy Opposition (give A/C position, time and altitude, and what happened) 15/L at 0138, 5000, near ~~CAMMON~~ ~~Ed~~ near VILLERS-LE GAMOON 50-11 N 04-38 E –

15. Weather. How did weather affect mission: In Route: Undercast made it difficult to find check At Target: points – at target weather was alright

16. Captains personal report Reception was good – weather on route not too good because of undercast weather at target was fine – Picked up Rebecca 25 miles 3000' ft.

D. J. Kaplan [illegible]
(INTERROGATION OFFICER)

COMMANDING OFFICER,
CARPETBAGGER PROJECT.

SECRET

Flight record of Playmate (BCRA record includes pigeons)

discipline. The standard procedure for German forces when capturing armed civilians in the area was to shoot them out of hand under the Hitler decree dealing with Partisans. General Eisenhower had attempted to give resistants some form of protection by declaring that they should be received as combatants and afforded the protection under the Geneva Convention for POWs, any diversion from these rules would be treated as a war crime.

On the 6th June it was announced that 300 men would be joining the Maquis Manise and that first day 70 men arrived and the following morning a further 90, bringing the total in the camp to over 190. The first few groups were fully equipped and what was issued had to be spread out. Again parachutes were used for tents and Desmond sent his first radio message back to London to warn them of the situation. In this telegram he made it clear that the men's tops were covered but not their bottoms. There was a deficiency in boots and trousers and the footwear that the men were turning up in was not strong enough for the conditions. He impressed the necessity for the immediate dispatch of trousers, shoes and warm clothing. Another item in seriously short supply was rucksacks, which made the movement of men and equipment difficult as everything had to be carried.

On this first day Captain Chavane, the intelligence officer Point, left the camp and went to Charleville to meet resistance chief Aubusson and to commence his duties and collate information about enemy forces and targets. He eventually built up an effective network of information gatherers in all the villages and towns in the area who fed information about German troop movements and forewarned of later attacks on the Maquis. He returned to the camp on the 11th June and unfortunately his network was not at that time sufficiently active to give forward information about an imminent German military action.

At about this time the resistance leaders started to motivate and recruit local men to join the Maquis in the forest. Resistance leader Fournier, who was proving to be less than helpful, even though he had been given specific instructions as to how he was to help the mission, was sending men to the forest and telling them that all their needs would be met by the mission. Men were turning up ill-equipped for a life in the woods and the mission's supplies were inadequate to meet all the needs. Another factor which became a problem was that the head of resistance for the town of Revin, Robert Charton, also started recruiting men for the Maquis using tactics which were both bullying and not in the best interests of the mission. Charton told all men that they must report to the mission in the forest and that they would be the subject of reprisals if they did not go. This, with the fervour which followed the news of the invasion, resulted in some 200 men and youths leaving Revin in large numbers, many on bicycles singing and waving flags patriotically. It did not take much for the Germans to realise that something was happening in the Manise forest north of Revin. Intelligence from informers of the gathering, together with the aerial reconnaissance, including photographs of the camp gave the German forces everything they needed to assess requirements for an offensive action against the Maquis.

Over the next few days Desmond sent a number of messages to get more equipment sent to the field and it was decided that to avoid over using Astrologie another drop site would be found. On the morning of the 12th June Desmond had been target shooting and demonstrating the specialist firearm he had brought to the field, the Welrod suppressed pistol. This weapon had been developed by SOE at the Inter-services Research Bureau also known as Station X. It was a bolt action magazine fed, single shot pistol with built in silencer and also known as the Assassin's Pistol, which speaks volumes about its designed purpose.

ATTACK

At 10 a.m. on 12th June the camp was visited by Fournier and Commandant René Derrien, a member of the General Staff for Region C (the Ardennes). René Derrien had been instructed to make an inspection of Citronelle's camp and he had a personal motive in that his son had joined this group and been appointed a group leader. René Derrien later made a complete report on his findings, but at the time he claimed he was critical of the location of the camp near to the roads and with the clearly defined paths leading to it. Smoke from camp fires burning green fuel was apparent and they entered the camp without being challenged. He also made the observation that there were too many men, many who had been press ganged and many who were treating the experience as a fun camp.

After the target practice Desmond and Victor Layton went off into the forest to locate another drop site which they had seen on the map about two miles north of the camp, they were in civilian clothes and armed with carbine rifles and pistols. There are conflicting reports of what happened; Layton states only that he and Desmond were together, other reports indicate there were some Maquis members nearby. Prof. M.R.D. Foot quotes a French source in a letter he wrote to a Canadian researcher, who claimed that there were Maquis members present near to Desmond and Layton. Having walked in this forest I find it difficult to believe that the two officers would wander off in this forest of tiny trails without taking guides with them for local knowledge. What is clear is that they were walking along a trail on the north side of the Manise River returning to camp just after midday when they heard gunfire coming from the direction of the camp. While they were determining the location of the camp a German soldier dressed in Field Grey uniform jumped from a hiding place behind bushes and shouted; "*Halt! Hände hoch!*" (Halt hands high).

The two men found themselves in a fight or flight situation, Layton reacted very quickly and ran into fir trees to his left. He fired his carbine and ducked under a shot from the German. He turned and shot this soldier and then made his escape. Layton reacted so quickly as he had been living in the field for two months at this stage and his survival instincts were well honed. Desmond faced a situation where he had firearms aimed at him and did not have time to unsling his carbine or draw his pistol. He chose to remain stationary and this had the effect of preventing the remaining German soldiers from chasing Layton and discovering the location of the camp (Desmond was unaware at this time that the location of the camp was known). If there were Maquis members present hidden behind other bushes as Prof. Foot's source claimed, then Desmond's reaction also saved their lives.

Layton returned to the camp to find that the presence in the forest of the German forces was known; patrols had been sent out and were returning with intelligence. A large scale search and attack operation had been mounted by 3,000 German troops under the command of the area Feldkommandantur commanded by Oberst Botho Rudolf Emil Wilhelm Grabowski.

This Officer was born in East Prussia in 1890 to a middle class German family; he was university educated and a product of the officer training system. He served throughout the First World War and was wounded twice. In December 1918 he was demobilised from the army but managed to secure an appointment with the German security police as a Captain in 1920. This organisation the Sicherheitspolizei was engulfed by the SS under the Nazis and came under the direct control of Heinrich Himmler and by December 1942 he had become a Kommandant of Feldkomandantur 545. In January 1943 was transferred in the same capacity to Charleville to head Feldkomandantur 684.

German military units in the Ardennes were very efficient and had managed to keep a tight control over the area; they consisted of Landesschütze Battalion 581. formed in 1941. This unit consisted of staff plus three companies of men. It was based in France during 1943 to 1944 with a HQ at Charleville-Mézières. Ost Battalion 680 (Russian) was originally from the eastern front, but from November 1943 was stationed in the Charleville area of the Ardennes and consisted of a mixture of Russian, Poles and other eastern country troops who had volunteered for service with the Wehrmacht to avoid the deprivations of the POW camps. They were led by German officers, armed with captured weapons and used mainly in anti-partisan activity.

Many accounts by local people after the event referred to the German forces as SS, but the officer used by Grabowski as a field commander for this assault was Major Theodor Molinari from an armoured formation that were traditionally dressed in black uniforms and easily mistaken for SS troops.

The patrols sent out from the Maquis camp reported that German forces had barred the roads out of Revin and were patrolling in vehicles along the forest roads and were stationed on the hilltops. The first contact was at 4 p.m. that day when a German patrol was fired upon and they retired having returned fire, hitting several Maquis members. The Maquis members dug large holes to bury food and ammunition, sporadic gunfire was heard from around the forest throughout the day. A decision was made to split the Maquis into three groups and escape at 11 p.m. This was partially successful but stragglers and inexperienced men found themselves lost and easy prey for the German soldiers to pick up. The German forces were camped along the road through the forest which led very close by the Maquis camp and a field next to a farmhouse at Les Vieux Moulins d'Hargnies was dedicated as a prisoner reception area. The family at this farm were locked in their house and told to keep their curtains closed and not look out. They did manage to get discreet views of proceedings and could hear what was being done to the prisoners. This was where Desmond was originally taken but when his identity as an Englishman was discovered he was removed to Oberst Grabowski's temporary headquarters.

Later on the first day the Citronelle mission, using the cover of the forest and darkness, commenced the logistically difficult process of moving the men and as much equipment as they could carry out of the German encirclement. The groups were split up but eventually the survivors re-grouped across the border in Belgium and continued their resistance activities from camps there.

Desmond's future lay in a very different direction.

PART VII

CAPTIVITY

REVIN

Desmond's captors took him to the temporary headquarters of Feldkomandantur 684, a large house on the road between Revin and Les Hautes-Buttes. This house was the local headquarters of the Todt organisation, which was the Nazi department responsible for construction and work including the conscription and supply of workers for the Reich.

Desmond was detained here from the 12th to 16th June, and interrogated in an effort to obtain information from him. The interrogation would have been about his identity and what organisation he belonged to, the identity of other members of the team and that of resistants. Of great interest to the Germans at this early stage was the strength of their opposition in respect of numbers, quality and arms. The issue of numbers was not in question as some 200 young men had left Revin to answer the call to arms, in a fashion which could not have gone unnoticed. However, this behaviour would indicate a lack of discipline and training, thereby indicating the calibre of opposition was willing but poor. The Germans were fully aware that men and arms had been dropped on or about 6th June and aerial reconnaissance had been conducted over the forest in an effort to locate the camps of the Maquis.

It is known that Desmond held out under violent interrogation and did not give the Germans any information. His SOE training was to hold out giving any information for the first 48 hours and to use delaying tactics in order to give those not in captivity time to move equipment and close down camps and safe houses. At one stage later on the 12th he was taken to the location where the captured resistants were being held and he was witnessed to be bruised from an obvious beating. At this stage he was now wearing his uniform battledress which had a chalk cross on his back, indicating he was marked for execution, as had other captured men and boys. From eyewitness accounts of other persons in the hands of Desmond's interrogators, it is probable that this visit to the field was to convince him that it was pointless for him to with hold information as they already had captives who were talking. Other captives had already given information resulting in the recovery of large quantities of arms, ammunition and stores, one account talks of five tons of stores having been recovered.

This technique had been used on a young man, Léon Uhl, who with all the other young men of Revin had cycled out to the forest to join the Maquis. On the night before the attacks began he had cycled back to Revin to spend the night with his wife, being newly married. He was stopped, arrested and interviewed about the location of the camp. He was persuaded to co-operate after being shown aerial photographs of the camp, identifiable due to the use of white parachutes used as tents to house the many men in the forest. Uhl agreed to come out to the location and was unfortunately seen in German company. Despite later escaping, returning to the company of the Maquis and fighting until liberation, he was put on trial post war, convicted of collaboration and sentenced to two years hard labour.

It was probable that this technique was being used on Desmond in an effort to convince him that there was no point in him holding back information. They also recovered with his battledress other personal possessions including the chess set brought with him from England. These items were given to him and remained in his possession throughout his time in captivity.

At this early stage of the operation the Germans were in possession of almost all of the information they needed to complete the operations against the Maquis, gathered from the resistants being held and tortured in the field. Desmond's most valuable secret to the Germans was who had received them when they had parachuted into France; this secret remained intact as the Fontaine family survived the war as did the other members of the mission.

CHARLEVILLE

On 16th June Desmond was moved to Charleville prison arriving at 1 p.m. and the surviving register shows him as prisoner 1309, a civilian. We know that he was housed in cell number one as an inscription was later found scratched into the cell wall:

Capt. Desmond Hubble,
109634,
British Army Intelligence Corps,
Brook House,
Moss Lane,
Pinner,
Middlesex.

This inscription was written down on a piece of paper and later given to George Whitehead in the course of his post war mission with Wing Commander Yeo-Thomas, Operation Outhaul (HS 6/372).

Interrogations of Desmond continued in Charleville prison and the detail given in this inscription show that the Germans knew, that any cover story he may have given was not of use, as he admits to being a member of the intelligence corps and his battledress had 'Intelligence Corps' shoulder flashes at the top of both sleeves. Any difference between the Intelligence Corps and the Intelligence Service would have made no difference to the Germans; he was arrested armed, behind the lines in civilian clothing and was in their eyes a terrorist. He also gave his parent's address, presumably in the hope that detail of his fate, so far, may be delivered to his family, a sure indicator that he had accepted that he was not going to be given the chance of treatment as a normal prisoner of war. Desmond used his cover story as prepared during the planning stages of the mission; these details are not recorded, but may have been along the lines that he was an escaped POW. He would not have been able to use the cover of downed allied aircrew as his battledress was incorrect and this story would only have been useful as a delaying tactic, as German records would soon be checked and the story shown to be false.

On 26th June Desmond's Charleville record shows that at 5 a.m. he was transferred to Saint-Quentin Prison, but there is no record that he arrived there. It is more probable looking at the map and the locations of the prisons in relationship to each other, that he was transferred directly to Fresnes Prison in Paris and this part of the entry is either a mistake or misinformation to make tracing his whereabouts difficult or impossible.

FRESNES PRISON

Fresnes prison was built from 1895 in the town of Fresnes, Val-de-Marne South of Paris. It is one of the largest prisons in France having 1,200 male cells and a small wing for women. It was the first of a radical design called the 'Telegraph Pole System' with a central corridor having secondary corridors running outwards from both sides of the centre.

The usual mode of transport to and from railway stations was purpose built prison vans with individual cells inside, the prisoners' wrists were secured in handcuffs behind their backs. On entry to the prison Desmond got out of the vehicle behind the main gates into a cobbled courtyard to the sound of German guards shouting abuse and encouragement to hurry. Any sign of slowness to react was met with physical abuse either by hand or rifle butts.

Following a prisoner roll check the prisoners were marched in line down corridors, through halls to be allocated to an individual cell. The cells were unlit, cold and of bleak stone construction. The steel constructed door fitted with a spyhole for the guards to monitor the inhabitant's movements and the walls containing scratched names, dates and messages from previous occupants. The cells were small and contained a toilet with small squares of newspaper, a wooden bed and a sink with a button operated tap. The only bedding was a much worn, threadbare, dirty blanket and a metal mug was provided for drinking and food. A window allowed daylight in and a view of prisoner holding and exercise pens, which were covered by a walkway for the guards to monitor the prisoners therein.

Various types of prisoner were housed at Fresnes. Ordinary prisoners included thieves, pimps and black marketeers. Military prisoners included shot down air crew both American and British and of course political prisoners such as French resistants and the likes of Desmond from SOE. This last category was deemed extremely dangerous from both the guard safety and escape points of view and when taken from cells were always shackled.

At the time Desmond was housed in Fresnes there were a large number of Allied aircrew inmates. They consisted of 168 American, British and Commonwealth flyers of both officer and NCO rank. These men had been incarcerated at Fresnes for periods from six days to nine months and were placed in cells in groups. They were constantly referred to as '*Terrorfliegers*' (terror fliers) and not sent to POW camps in accordance with the Geneva Convention. They were also transported by train to Buchenwald concentration camp after Desmond, but before the liberation of Paris. In later testimony the fliers described the conditions in Fresnes stating there was a constant stream of cries and screams of people being abused and tortured. On frequent occasions the men heard shots and believed that people had been executed. Some of the airmen were taken outside and placed against bullet marked walls and the guards pretended to form a firing squad, merely for their own amusement. The guards were German Wehrmacht and of a nature not suited to frontline duty such as those who served in the first war, but all had in common an ability to be both verbally and physically brutal in their treatment of the prisoners. Those that ever showed any kindness to prisoners did so when not accompanied by their peers, indicating that the regime expected them to be brutal.

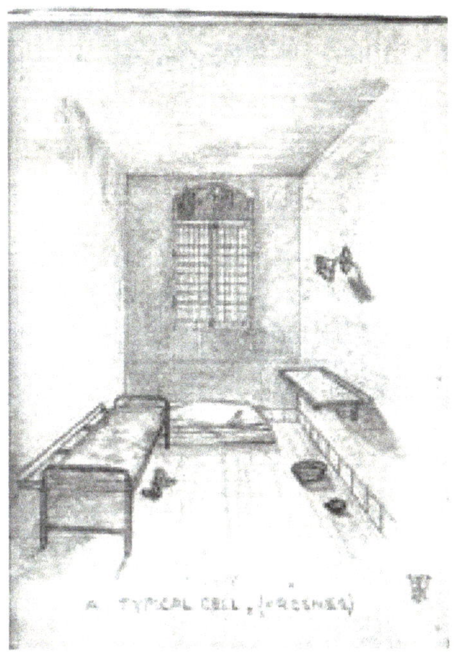

Sketch of a Fresnes cell made by unknown allied airman

Sustenance for Desmond's category of prisoner was water from the sink tap, a mug of Ersatz coffee for breakfast (a coffee substitute made from acorns or roasted chicory), a slice of soggy bread for lunch (probably containing sawdust for greater bulk) and a mug of turnip based soup for evening meal. Coffee and soup were delivered to each cell from a metal trolley running on a railing system along the corridors, operated by a prisoner trustee accompanied by a German guard. Failure on a prisoner's or trustee's behalf to act quickly in holding out his mug was rewarded by physical and verbal abuse by the guard. One condition commonly suffered by the prisoners was flea bites; the prison suffered from an infestation likely to be caused by straw or horse hair filled mattresses.

Various methods of communication were available to prisoners ranging from shouting or singing from cell to cell, removing the button operating the tap and speaking to an adjoining cell through the pipework or removing a small pane of glass in the window and calling to prisoners from opposite wings. Communication between prisoners was banned and resulted in a beating for those caught. Caution had to be observed at all times as prisoners were encouraged to become *stool pigeons* for the Gestapo and spies were planted in an effort to extract more information under the guise of being a fellow inmate. One communication method Desmond did use was to ask his jailors for a bible. After this was provided he placed coded messages inside and asked for the bible to be passed on, which ultimately would be returned with replies. One of the objectives of Operation Outhaul (HS6/372), undertaken after the cessation of hostilities in Europe by Wing Commander Yeo Thomas and Squadron Leader George Whitehouse, was to locate these bibles at Fresnes, unfortunately without success. The main successes of Outhaul were to finalise payments to Yeo-Thomas's contacts within his Parisian group and to identify and locate potential witnesses for war crimes trials in respect of Fresnes and two concentration camps (the story of which is to follow) and to locate where Desmond had been taken to after arrest in the Ardennes, (Cell no 1 Charleville). This file also indicates in George Whitehead's report that Desmond and Yeo-Thomas were in Fresnes at the same time and the bible communication was with each other. The two main accounts of Yeo-Thomas's experience state that they first met again on the train to Buchenwald, but at the time of Outhall Yeo-Thomas was suffering the effects of his experiences at the hands of the Nazi's and information must be viewed with circumspect.

Whilst in custody at Fresnes it is likely that Desmond was taken to the local Gestapo headquarters at 82-86 Avenue Foch and interrogated there. Post war accounts from survivors incarcerated with Desmond, state that he was tortured and beaten but the specifics were never recorded. The German intelligence service probably knew all it needed to know about Desmond's mission from captured resistants at Revin; however, there still would have been interest in him from a desire to learn more about SOE, its contacts, training and operational methods. The Gestapo had previously had huge successes gained from the interrogation and breaking of agents and resistants. In Paris alone the Prosper circuit had been broken resulting in the arrest of over 1,500 people, many of whom never saw their families or homeland again. From the accounts of interrogations held at Avenue Foch the techniques ranged from easy casual chats to extremes of violence depending on whether the subject was being cooperative or not. Holding cells were located on the top floor of this HQ and other rooms were equipped for various types of torture such as a bath to continually and partially drown a subject. By this time Desmond was in a position to avoid torture, by using delaying tactics such as agreeing with confronted facts and giving useless information, such as spent intelligence and deception to his inquisitors. Accounts given by those who survived state they had a desire to save the relatives of their comrades the awful detail of what their loved ones suffered, but they also had a strong desire for revenge and justice against the perpetrators of these atrocities. Official records have no details other than that he was beaten badly during interrogation, the issue of torture is anecdotal among other accounts.

On the 8th of August 1944 Desmond was transferred from Fresnes Prison to Gare de l'este and placed on a train bound for Germany, destination Buchenwald. On 24th August 1944 Paris was declared an open city once again and surrendered to allied forces. Before the final liberation many resistants not placed on trains were murdered in Fresnes prison by the Gestapo rather than allow them to become witnesses of war crimes.

THE ROAD TO BUCHENWALD

The Nazis classified prisoners such as Desmond as dangerous terrorists and they had a policy called, 'Nacht und Nebel' (NN) meaning 'Night and Fog', to deal with them in a special way. Those classified in this way were to simply disappear, destined for concentration camps and execution. The policy had its origins in a decree issued by Hitler on 7th December 1941, designed to simplify the way people who had undermined the security of German troops in occupied countries were dealt with. He had decided that existing military measures to deal with this issue were too lenient and took too much time. This decree made it possible for people to simply disappear straight to Germany where special courts would deal with them harshly. Records were simply marked NN and no indication as to where they went or what had happened to them was kept. This was intended as a terror tactic to create fear in the populations that control was sought over. In July 1944 the decree was extended to include all violent acts, perpetrated by non-German people in occupied countries, to be treated as terrorists and those not summarily executed were to be handed to the security police. This was then extended to cover all acts contrary to German interests, which basically meant that anyone doing anything to the annoyance of the Germans could simply be made to disappear marked 'NN'.

At the railway station Desmond was placed in a wagon with two compartments, the windows and corridor wall were covered in bars. Each compartment was designed for eight persons to sit, but the seats had been removed to create more space. In Desmond's compartment there were 18 prisoners, manacled in pairs, some were military officers and others were French Resistants. In the compartment opposite there were a further 18 prisoners similarly shackled, making a total of 36 prisoners. Before the train set off a further prisoner was added to the compartment opposite and Desmond saw that this addition was his friend Yeo-Thomas who had been moved from Fresnes to Compiegne prison when his file had gone missing and he had been mistaken for a low category prisoner. The mistake had been noticed and rectified placing Yeo-Thomas back onto the road to Germany.

Coincidentally, amongst the other SOE agents on the train with Desmond was Captain Charles Rechenmann of F section. Rechenmann was arrested on 10th May 1944 at Angouleme, South West France whilst operating with the Rover circuit which had been infiltrated. Desmond had been originally assigned to the Rover circuit but was transferred to Citronelle when it was discovered that Rover had been compromised.

Another strange twist of fate occurred on this first day of the journey; in another section of the carriage were women prisoners, two of which were SOE agents, Noor Inayat Khan and Violette

Szabo. The latter had been captured after a fire fight with German soldiers in June 1944 a few days after parachuting into France for the same purpose as Desmond. Whether Desmond knew her or not we cannot know but Szabo was later murdered at Ravensbruck concentration camp almost to the same day as Desmond died and was later awarded a posthumous George Cross. As I have previously mentioned, in 1958 a film relating her story was released and the starring role was played by Virginia McKenna who as a small girl had met Desmond at her home in South Africa.

By the afternoon of the first day the prisoners were still manacled together in their cells and no one had been to the toilet or given any food or water. A German speaking French agent Stephane Hessel, who was locked in with Yeo-Thomas, negotiated with a guard to allow the prisoners to go to the toilet in their pairs. During the course of this function the 37 men were able to see who was also sharing the same train journey. This also allowed a short respite to the cramped conditions as there was insufficient space in each compartment for everyone to sit down at the same time and a rota had to be arranged between standing and sitting.

To give an insight into the brutality with which the guards assigned to this type of duty were likely to treat their charges, when the 168 allied aircrew were transported from Fresnes, on a later train destined also for Buchenwald, an incident occurred which was related in the testimony of Squadron Leader P.J. Lamason DFC and bar RNZAF. He reported that he and the other prisoners were placed in rail goods wagons with French civilians 89 per car. The only ventilation was a grilled opening in the front and rear walls of the wagon. When a French male prisoner placed his hands on the bars a guard shot him in the hand. The train was then stopped and the prisoner was dragged outside by the guards who were shouting abuse at him, he was made to walk away from the carriage and an officer shot him with his pistol in the middle of his back. As the man's body was twitching on the floor a guard shot him with a machine-pistol. Two of the aircrew prisoners were given a shovel and made to bury the victim at the side of the railway.

Any thoughts of escape that the prisoners may have countenanced to date had been stopped by the manner of their transport and the level of guardianship provided by the German guards. Perhaps they thought that their only chance may come in an air raid, if they did their thoughts were answered as the train was attacked from the air and strafed with machine gun bullets and canon shells. Following an explosion the train rolled to a halt and the guards' attention was now trained on the attacking aircraft which they had engaged from the side of the train with machine guns. During the attack two of the women including Violette Szabo, neglected their own safety and potential opportunity to escape in order to crawl along the carriage with some water giving the men a much needed drink. This act of bravery was depicted in the film as mentioned and was no doubt scripted from the statements of witness survivors.

When the air raid was over the train remained stationary for some hours which in the August sun made conditions in the train unbearably hot. Eventually some trucks arrived alongside the train and the prisoners were taken off and loaded, men to one and women to the other. Any hopes of an opportunity to escape were dashed when one of the guards threatened to shoot all the prisoners in the event of anyone escaping. This created a difficult situation and factions in the prisoners between those with a sense of duty and desire to escape and those with a more recalcitrant attitude. After a brief stop at a town called Charlons-sur-Marne, where the prisoners were able to drink and wash in a fountain, the night was spent in the stables of a military barracks at Verdun. The men were placed in one row of stalls and the women in a separate row in an effort to keep them apart. A few short conversations were possible and as shown in the film, *Carve Her Name with Pride* Violette Szabo was able to speak briefly with her SOE mentor, Harry Peuleve. Violette was the widow of a French aviator killed in North Africa, they had a daughter, but due to her command of the French language she came to the notice of SOE and was recruited as an agent. Violette and Harry Peuleve fell in love whilst training so the reunion in such awful circumstances was a blessing and a tragedy all in one. Violette's daughter wore a pretty dress, which her mother had bought in Paris on a previous mission, on the day she was taken to Buckingham Palace by her Grandfather to be awarded her mother's posthumous George Cross.

The following morning the prisoners were unshackled, probably in limited numbers for security purposes and allowed to wash. When they were again secured ready to continue the journey, Hubble found he was now shackled to Yeo-Thomas.

Following Desmond's interview with Yeo-Thomas for transfer to RF section the two men became firm friends and Yeo-Thomas had appreciated the support shown him by various people in connection with his difficulties in obtaining logistical support for their work. Two of those friends specifically mentioned by Yeo-Thomas are Desmond and George Whitehead.

The journey continued in the trucks but the men and women now took different directions. The women were taken to various locations and ultimately Inayat Khan was murdered in Dachau Concentration Camp and Violette Szabo was murdered at Ravensbruck. This leg of the men's journey took them over the border from France into Germany. The likelihood of any escape attempt was now becoming more and more remote, as they were now in enemy country and would not be able to seek help and refuge from the population. Being shackled to a friend with the same sense of duty and courage was a morale boosting opportunity. Just before the town of Saarbrucken the truck turned into Neue Bremm Concentration Camp and stopped.

NEUE BREMM CONCENTRATION CAMP

Neue Bremm Straflager had been built in 1943 by the Saarbrucken Gestapo and under the control of SS-Untersturmfuhrer fritz Schmoll who was now the Commandant until November 1944. Schmoll was a firm believer in the use of extreme brutality and violence and had built a regime of fear designed to break a prisoner's spirit in a very short time, as all executions and punishments were done in full view of the inmates. The prison had been built with the intention of keeping inmates for a short period before their release, or transportation to other camps such as Buchenwald and had a cross section of inmates including criminals, political opponents of the Nazis, Jews and resistants. Between 1943 and 1945 hundreds of inmates from 14 different countries were killed in this camp, Schmoll was tried as a war criminal, convicted and executed in 1946.

Desmond and the other 36 prisoners soon found out just how barbaric conditions were in a Gestapo controlled camp. As he and Yeo-Thomas alighted from the truck they were set upon and beaten by guards using short rubber truncheons. All the men were lined up, receiving beatings in the process and then shackled in five man groups, four men forming a square with one in the centre. The system of shackling the prisoners in a five man group was for the amusement of the guards who roared with laughter at the attempts of the men to coordinate themselves. It was part of the process designed to humiliate and break any spirit of resistance the men may have had left. The shackles were only removed when the guards tired of this abuse. They were then shackled back in pairs and locked in a small wooden hut less than 10 ft. square. In the hut they were given an oil drum for a toilet and their only excursions from the hut were to empty the drum and to collect food. The only furniture in the hut was a narrow shelf around part of the walls and the roof was made of metal creating a sweltering heat and unbearable conditions for the inhabitants. There was insufficient room for all of the men to sit or lie and again a rota system had to be developed and turns taken to sit, lie down or lean against a wall. Another systematic abuse they suffered was, when they were called for food they had to collect their rations via guards who beat them on the way and then sent them back before they could finish and tripped them up so what food left was lost.

The men were kept at this camp for three to four days whilst transport was arranged and in this time they witnessed other prisoners especially Jews, being treated in a bestial manner. Prisoners became animal-like in an effort to avoid beatings or worse. On witnessing this treatment of the inmates, Desmond mentioned to Yeo-Thomas:

"If this is an example of German Kultur, the sooner the bastards are wiped out the better." (Direct quote, The Bravest of the Brave by Mr. Mark Seaman).

Hope of a brighter future was given on the day they were paraded, placed on transports and taken to Saarbrucken railway station under the guardianship of a detachment of Wehrmacht Feldgendarmen with a Hauptman in charge. The hope of a place in a prisoner of war camp was re-ignited by better travelling conditions when they were placed in a goods wagon with space for them all to lie down at once and with a good flow of fresh air. Three guards were in the wagon with them which gave rise to thoughts of overpowering them and escaping from the train. The negative minded again put a stop to any attempt and threatened to inform the guards in an effort to save their own lives. By this time Yeo-Thomas had established himself as the most senior officer of the prisoners and thereby the right to lead and give orders. He had appointed Desmond as his right hand man, as the two men saw eye to eye and Yeo-Thomas knew that he could rely at all times on Desmond's support and counsel. Initially he had overruled the dissenters and had given his approval for the escape attempt by the 12 willing to try, but eventually he had to give in as the plan was doomed to failure by the attitude of the reluctant few.

During the course of the journey the prisoners were transferred from the goods van to a third class carriage where they were again convinced of a brighter future. Desmond, as a German speaker, was able to have a conversation with the captain commanding the security detail about their destination. It turned out that this officer knew his distant relative, Julius Kayser, with whom Desmond and his wife had holidayed in 1937 for three weeks on Kayser's vineyards on the Moselle at Traben-Trarbach. This officer informed them that they were destined not for a POW camp but to a special camp which provided some very nice facilities for them. He described a band playing music, a multi-lingual library, a theatre and cinema, a well-equipped hospital and good food, all these facilities existed but not for Desmond and his companions.

In his memoirs Harry Peuleve noted that he did not think the officer was trying to hoodwink them, but that the propaganda put out by Joseph Goebbels and his ministry had been believed. It is quite amazing that the truth of the concentration camps under the Nazis was hidden, by the veil of secrecy surrounding the camps and the propaganda peddled to the German people and the world. Even those German citizens living in close proximity to the camps and who often benefited from the criminal profit making of the camp administrations, either did not know the truth or chose to ignore the very obvious.

At about 12 midnight on Wednesday 16th August 1944 the train pulled into Weimar railway station where the prisoners' carriage was uncoupled and shunted onto a siding surrounded by a barbed wire enclosure. After handing over guardianship of the prisoners to the SS guards, the Feldgendarmerie withdrew and Desmond now found himself and his comrades at the mercy of one of the most brutal prison systems ever to be devised, Konzentrationslager Buchenwald and the SS.

PART VIII

BUCHENWALD CONCENTRATION CAMP

(KONZENTRATIONSLAGER BUCHENWALD, KLB)

HISTORY

The first concentration camps set up by the Nazi regime opened in 1933 immediately following Hitler's appointment as Chancellor. The first inmates of these camps were drunks, wife beaters and other persons deemed social misfits by the authorities such as union representatives and political opponents of Hitler. The terms served by these victims varied from a few months to permanent incarceration and were intended as a programme of re-education. The inmates were put through a tough physical exercise programme including brutal treatment by their guards. Those lucky enough to be released were sworn to silence about the camps and their treatment under threat of being returned to prison, not many broke their silence! Approximately 45,000 people were incarcerated under this scheme.

In 1934/5 the organisation of the camps was transferred to the SS under the direct control of Heinrich Himmler and at this stage only 3,000 people were still imprisoned. The camp system was greatly expanded and used to further Hitler's aim of ridding German society of those he saw as racially undesirable such as Jews and Gypsies.

In July 1937 149 prisoners, mainly political prisoners and criminals, were brought to the site of a proposed new camp near to the Town of Weimar and put to work constructing what was initially called Konzentrationslager Ettersberg. The site chosen was on the side of the Ettersburg Mountain in a Beech forest and the name was soon changed to the literal translation of Beech forest, Buchenwald. Stone was cut and used from a nearby quarry and wood from the forest. Prisoners assigned to the quarry were subjected to a brutal regime and made to carry each stone to where it was needed. If the stone chosen by the prisoner was deemed too small by the guards the prisoner was beaten unmercifully. This left a choice for the prisoner of carrying a stone heavier than required and risking using too much energy or choosing one too small and risking a beating. The main camp was built in a fan shape expanding out from a main entrance of metal gates surrounded by a building the left of which was a punishment block and to the right administration buildings. Atop the gates was a watch tower with machine guns mounted in such a position to command a field of fire covering the fan shaped camp. On the outside of the watchtower a large clock was mounted in the wall greeting prisoners with their time of arrival.

Very few female prisoners were kept at Buchenwald, the first were 20 political prisoners shipped there from Ravensbruck concentration camp in 1941. These women were forced to form a brothel at Buchenwald, which continued throughout the life of the camp and was staffed by volunteers from Ravensbruck who were enticed on the promise of better rations. There were less than 1,000 women inmates in total.

The camp comprised two separate camps, the Little Camp and Big Camp. The accommodation of the little camp were tents, situated conveniently near to the crematorium, and was largely inhabited by Jews and those who the Nazis wanted to die quickly. Conditions were poor and the food rations set at starvation levels with one bowl of thin soup per person and a loaf of bread between eight prisoners per day. The big camp was where the general population was housed and the accommodation made of wooden block houses sitting on concrete bases.

The first commandant appointed to Buchenwald was SS Standartenführer (Colonel) Karl-Otto Koch on 1st August 1937. Koch had a large mansion built for him and his wife Ilse who was a keen horse rider and riding stables were also built for her pleasure. In these stables a false infirmary was built with a height measuring instrument against a wall. Prisoners would be stood against the measure and from the other side of the wall a guard with a pistol shot them in the back of the head through a hole. The sound of the shot was disguised by a loud radio. It is estimated that 8,000 Russian POW's were murdered in this fashion at Buchenwald. Camp guard Horst Dittrich, giving evidence at the post war Buchenwald war crimes trial, claimed that the victims were Political Commissars, executed under a Hitler order which demanded the execution of these men in reprisal for atrocities committed against German troops, in particular SS on the eastern front.

Between 1937 and 1939 all bodies were taken to Weimar and disposed of in the town's crematorium, this was obviously at a cost to the camp's funds. In 1939 a small crematorium was built in the camp, but as the daily death toll rose the small crematorium became inadequate. In 1942 a larger facility was built with six ovens made by Topf & Sons in nearby Erfurt. Beneath the floor where the ovens stood was a room used for executions, which had hooks attached high up on the wall. There are many stories describing the use of these hooks and the means of hanging the bodies and it is likely that all these stories are true. The original purpose was probably to hang dead bodies to ensure they became straight thereby facilitating placing the body into the oven with ease. A large cosh was on hand to smash the skull of any prisoner showing signs of life. A lift from this room was used to get the bodies up to the furnaces for disposal.

Also built in the camp was a cinema theatre where films of Nazi propaganda were shown. Following the Normandy landings of 6th June film footage taken by German film makers was shown in the theatre, but the truth that the landings were successful was hidden and the films only showed American GIs being machine gunned and tanks and other equipment destroyed. The inmates were issued with tickets which had printed on the reverse, '*Disziplin, mehr disziplin, immer mehr disziplin*'. ('Discipline, more discipline, always more discipline'). This theatre also served as a rehearsal room for the camp band.

Every evening from 6.30 p.m. a band played military marches just outside the main gate entrance to welcome home the returning inmates who had been on work kommandos in the factories built outside the camp. One such factory was Gustloff-Werk 2 where components for the V2 rockets were made. The prisoners chosen to work in these factories were usually tradesmen whose trade gave them nimble fingers. This particular detail was seen as very desirable as an extra mug of thin soup was added to the daily ration for each inmate. Another factory made firearms and a supply of weapons were stolen piece by piece and kept at the camp by an underground resistance movement who were waiting for the right time to rise up and liberate themselves.

There was a hospital for prisoners but any inmates entering rarely came back out again. A section of this hospital was used to experiment on prisoners with vaccines for cholera, spread by lice and a problem for these overcrowded camps. Prisoners, usually French, were actually injected with cholera and then studied while they spent days on end dying in delirious agony. On one occasion another experiment was to inject four Russian prisoners with a poison to determine a fatal dosage, when they did not die they were taken to the crematorium execution room, hung and then dissected to determine why the poison had not killed them.

Commandant Koch had served in the army during World War 1, receiving the Iron Cross 2nd class for bravery and the Wound Medal (grade black). He was captured by the British in 1918 and spent the rest of the war as a prisoner himself. After returning to Germany he worked as a supervisor in both banking and insurance and joined the Nazi party and SS in 1931. In 1935 he became commandant of the Columbia concentration camp in Berlin, 10 months later he transferred as commandant of Esterwegen and then four months later to Sachsenhausen. Ilse Koch was unique as a commandant's wife; she was given authority over prisoners and guards giving orders as if from her husband. Husband and wife grossly abused their positions, creating a system of self-enrichment. Ilse Koch rode around the prisoner compounds often wearing provocative clothing and when a prisoner looked at her she either ordered him whipped or took his number and reported the incident to her husband for him to have the man whipped. In either case this would be 25 lashes on bare buttocks whilst the victim was pinned to a purpose made whipping stool. It was also alleged that she had a fascination for tattoos and had tattooed men murdered, the skin flayed and cured to make lamp-shades, photo albums, bags and other personal possessions. A subsequent SS enquiry failed to find evidence of these allegations nor did a later war crimes trial, however the Koch's were aware of an impending SS investigation into their activities at the camp and had plenty of opportunity to dispose of physical evidence. There is plenty of eye witness testimony and a few relics to state that these allegations were no doubt true.

Commandant Koch set to with creating a brutal regime for the prisoners and exploitation for personal financial gain from the camp. A canteen was provided and prisoners given tokens for work but there was rarely anything to buy. The camp had production facilities around it and provided labour to work in these factories, the profits should have all been paid to SS funds but Koch filtered off money for himself. Red Cross parcels for the prisoners were sold to German residents from Weimar and the funds pocketed and the prisoners themselves were robbed of possessions on arrival or made to pay bribes for better conditions or transfer elsewhere. The spoils of these activities were kept by the Commandant and his wife and not shared with underlings, thereby amassing personal fortunes and also enemies. In September 1941 Koch was moved to be Commandant of Majdanek Concentration Camp, by this time both he and Ilse Koch were under SS investigation for murder and embezzlement. Koch fell from grace and was eventually shot by an SS firing squad in Buchenwald in April 1945 one week before the camp was liberated.

Koch was replaced by Oberführer Hermann Pister who proved to be as brutal a man as his predecessor and remained the Buchenwald Commandant until liberation.

A rail link from Weimar was brought to the camp and a road built from the railway station to the gatehouse entrance. This road was subsequently named by the prisoners as 'Caracho Weg' as the expectation of the prisoners was to double time march from the platform to the camp gates. A graphic description of the arrival of prisoners at this station is given by Louis Gros in his memoirs written with Flint Whitlock, 'Survivor of Buchenwald: My Personal Odyssey'. He describes that after a nightmare three day, two night train journey from Compiegne in France where the men were packed tight into cattle trucks with little water and no food, the train stopped and the men were ordered out of the cars by shouting SS guards. A lorry arrived to take the dead away who had died either due to the cramped conditions or had been murdered by the guards. The survivors were made to line up and all the time the SS were shouting and beating them with sticks. Women, assumed to be SS wives, were nearby to enjoy the spectacle of this humiliation of the men, many of whom were not fully dressed. When some sort of order was established the men were forced to run up the road to the camp gates which a sentry opened to admit them. On the gates in metal lettering were the words, '*Jedem Das Seine*' (To Each His Own) and '*Recht Oder Unrecht Mein Vaterland*' (Right or Wrong My Country).

THE GUARDS AND ADMINISTRATION

The German Camp and extermination system was planned and run with the minimum of manpower. For the extermination of the Jews in the east, local populations were encouraged to take vengeance on their Jewish neighbours and afterwards finished by Einsatzgruppen supplemented by local militias. The organisation of Jewish populations into ghettos and subsequent transportation to either extermination or work camps was made much easier by lies and deceit on a gargantuan scale, in order to ensure that the intended victims were compliant. Buchenwald was no different, the German guards were of the *SS*-Totenkopfverbände (SS-TV) or Deaths Head Units, but inmates were then used to increase the manpower control of the prisoners. In immediate control of inmates were Kapos, usually German criminal prisoners who were encouraged to be brutal to their charges. They were issued with an armband to signify position and a rope cosh to administer beatings with. If a camp guard decided that a Kapo was being lenient, he would beat the Kapo, who then also ran the risk of having their status removed, thereby losing privileges and then being at the mercy of those they had previously been in charge of. Needless to say self-preservation took over and the Kapos were rarely anything other than brutal to their charges.

In charge of the accommodation blocks was a blockalteste whose duties were the discipline of prisoners, hygiene and the distribution of food. They held office with power and did not have to work with the prisoners. It was a sought after post due to the privileges and the opportunity to have extra food. In overall charge of all departments was a Lagerälteste or camp elder.

The administrations of the camp was largely done by prisoners and at first German criminals were used, but eventually all these tasks were taken over by communists, as their ranks were full of useful workers and their organisational ability was better. These posts were highly influential and made decisions on who was assigned to which jobs and barracks. It was unwise to tell the communist administrators on arrival at the camp that you had been a manager or business owner, as this would usually destine that individual to the worst jobs.

Louis Gros relates how he passed signs stating the 10 commandments of the camp and warning signs of danger that the fencing was electrically charged. Various other signs made motivational statements such as, 'Es gibt einen weg zur freiheit', (There is a way to Freedom). He remembers a zoo which was built for the entertainment of the SS and their families, an SS petrol station and a 'vainglorious' Nazi eagle carved out of a solid block of white granite. Through the gates was the appellplatz (roll call place) where the prisoners were paraded twice a day for roll call. On this first day Gros and the others were lined up and the lorry that had collected the dead from the train pulled up in front of them. The dead bodies of two young Frenchmen who had been shot for attempting to escape from the train were placed behind the rear wheels of the lorry, which then reversed backwards and forwards over them leaving the burst corpses for all to see.

The first parade was at 4 a.m. every day and those prisoners that had died in the night were brought out to be counted with the living to ensure that the numbers tallied. These roll calls were conducted in all weathers and the inmates were required to stand to attention throughout the process. Failure to stand still resulted in a beating or worse. If, as often happened the numbers did not tally, the count was done again and again until the correct figure was achieved. The prisoners were then marched away for their work detail of the day.

Gatehouse Entrance (Photo Mr J. Isaac)

ARRIVAL

This was the hell that existed when Desmond and the other 36 prisoners arrived in Buchenwald, which by now housed approximately 82,000 people due to the camps inmate numbers being swollen by the German army's retreat to Germany from the east. The gates were swung open and the men entered and any hopes of admission to a POW camp must have disappeared by this time. The guards started shouting at the prisoners in German, knocking caps off heads and stamping them into the ground as if the caps had offended them. They were then marched passed the lines of huts and taken into a large hall and handed over to members of the camp police. These were prisoners in striped uniforms wearing black armbands with the title Lagerschutz on them, another example of the Nazi's use of prisoners to ease their own burden.

They were held in this location until early morning with no information or refreshments. During this period of uncertainty as to their future or even what sort of place they had been delivered to one of the Lagerschutz, who spoke good English, told them they were destined for immediate '*special treatment*' and orders had been received that they were to be taken to the crematorium for execution. By the early hours of the morning it became apparent that immediate execution was not going to happen as they were taken to the delousing station.

Lice were a major concern for concentration camp administrations as they were the carriers of typhus and great lengths were taken to prevent an outbreak. This is rather ironic as they were more than happy to inject prisoners with the disease in a controlled environment, but feared a random outbreak. The prisoners were made to empty their pockets, contents placed into bags and their clothing removed and hung enclosed in large paper sacks. They were issued with a metal disc by means of a receipt and their possessions were removed to the Effektenkammer.

The next room contained a number of white coated barbers who shaved the men from head to foot with clippers, then they were doused in disinfectant which burnt the skin and handed a small quantity of soap. The next room had hundreds of sprinklers in the ceiling and hot water was turned on for the men to shower. After washing they were issued with wooden clogs and a mixture of camp uniform, a striped suit and ill-fitting random civilian clothes. Each man was given a number and an identifying badge made of cloth to sew onto their jackets.

The badge system differed from prisoner to prisoner depending upon their antecedents. Most badges were triangular in shape and of different colours, pink for homosexuals, green for criminals, purple for Jehovah's Witnesses and red for political prisoners. These badges were worn inverted but in the case of POWs and spies the red triangle was worn point up. The other shape used was for Jewish prisoners and they were given two triangles, worn one over the other, or one inverted and the other point up, to form the Star of David. These were yellow but in the case of a mixed history the colours were blended, for instance a Jewish homosexual had one yellow and one pink triangle.

Desmond was issued with the prisoner number 14930 and whilst they were being issued with clothing they were approached by an English speaking prisoner who introduced himself as Lieutenant Maurice Pertschuk of F section. Pertschuk was using the name Martin Perkins in the camp and in fact was Jewish. He had been captured in April 1943 having entered France a year earlier to organise the Prunus Circuit in the Toulouse area. Given up to the Gestapo by an informer he had been tortured by the infamous Klaus Barbie, 'The Butcher of Lyon', before being sent to Paris and then on to Buchenwald. Pertschuk warned the men that they were in the worst of German camps, that the treatment and mortality rate was appalling and that they must be very careful. The camp was full of informers who were willing to sell their fellow inmates for food or more favourable treatment and they should be very careful of what they told the camp administrators of their personal antecedents. The administrators at this time were communists and were responsible for the allocation of work to all the inmates. It could be a fatal mistake to admit to being an officer or an industrialist, as either would mark you for a work kommando of such an arduous nature as to be a death sentence. Desmond had already made a conscious decision to be defiant and to show his captors that he was a British officer and that he had not been beaten. He gave his rank as Captain and his profession as Company Director, recorded by the clerk as Kfm. Direktor (Company director).

RECORDS AND ADMISSION

The camp records show the following details given by the prisoners;

Politisch Franzosen		Lagerstuf. III
1. 8511 Allard, Elisse	14.7.16 Vieux Conde	Offizier
2. 7859 Avallart, Jean	17.12.08 Granville	Berufsoffizier
3. 13092 Benoist, Robert	20.3.95 Ramboullet	Ingenieur
4. 7864 Beuguennee, Jean	25.7.12 St. Eley	Journalist
5. 10375 Chaigneau, Jacques	18.2.23 Cap St. Jacques	Offizier
6. 9548 Culiole, Pierre	20.7.12 Brest	Berufsoffizier
7. 8870 Defendini, Ange	4.12.09 Ile du Salut	Berufsoffizier
8. 7795 Evesque, Jean	16.12.09 Paris	Offizier
9. 8144 Frager, Henri	3.3.97 Paris	Architeckt
10. 8051Garry, Emile	2.4.09 Vierzon	Ingeniur
11. 7582 Gerard, Rene	22.6.11 Bar le Duo	Gerichtsvollz
12. 7570 Guillot, Bernard	29.10.13 Dijon	Unteroffizier
13. 10033 Hessel,	20.10.17 Paris	Student
14. 10381 Heusch, Henri	29.11.09 Paris	Offizier
15. 10092 Keunen, Marcel	30.5.11 Neerpelt	Beamter
16. 15374 Leccia, Marcel	1.1.11 Ajaccio	Autovertreter
17. 10045 Lavallee, Jean	1.10.13 Saint Nazaire	Marineoffizier
18. 7638 Loison, Yves 1	14.3.21 La Mans	Flieger
19. 13474 Mulsant, Pierre	13.7.14 Villefranche	Spediteur
20. 7436 Rambaud, Christian	17.9.13 Paris	Offizier
21. 8945 Rechenmann, Charles	24.8.12 St Louis le Ritsch	Ingenieur
22. 11491 de Seguier, Jean	27.3.18 Paris	Berufsoffizier
23. 8900 Southgate, Maurice	20.6.13 Paris	Dekorateur
24. 10253 Vellaut, Paul	27.12.07 St. Ame	Berufsoffizier

Politisch Englander		**Lagerstuf. 111**
25. 10449 Barret, Denis	23.11.15 Velembes	Schneider
26. 14624 Dodkin, Kenneth	17.6.01 London	Buchprüfer
27. 14930 Hubble, Desmond	29.1.10 London	Kfm. Direktor
28. 12463 Kane, Gerald	10.8.11 Tiverton	Privatangest
29. 9636 Macalister, John	9.7.14 Guelph	Advocat
30. 9191 Mayer, James	9.4.20 Madagaskar	Fabrikdirektor
31. 12332 Peuleve, Henry	29.1.16 Worthing	Ingenieur
32. 8738 Sabourin, Guy	1.1.23 Montreal	Offizier
33. 7898 Steele, Arthur	6.4.21 Noeux les	Musiker
34. 7740 Wilkinson, George	31.8.13 Paris	Hotelier
Politisch Kanadier.		**Lagerstuf. 111**
35. 9992 Pickersgill, Frank	28.5.15 Winnepeg	Leutnant
Politisch Belgier.		**Lagerstuf. 111**
36. 12817 Detal, Julien	2.5.15 Maison Lafitte	Offizier
37. 14185 Gelen, Pierre	24.6.16 Rothem	Monteur

Reproduced from a copy of Buchenwald Camp Memorial records.

BLOCK SEVENTEEN

The men were then marched to a long wooden hut, block 17 which was enclosed within its own wire fence to isolate it from the rest of the camp. The hut was smaller than the rest and used to house special prisoners whom the SS guards wished to keep out of contact with the rest of the inmates. This was probably to keep within the policy of 'Nacht und Nebel' leaving no trace as to where the prisoners were disposed of. The entrance to the hut led to the latrine and wash area, doorways on either side led to the sleeping quarters one way and the living area another. The sleeping quarters consisted of tiers of wooden bunks on both sides sufficient for 40 men. With the inmates already housed there this made the quarters very overcrowded and Desmond chose to share a bunk with his friend Yeo-Thomas. The two men were now becoming very close; their friendship now sealed by this shared horrific experience.

Floor to ceiling bunks in Buchenwald.
(courtesy scrapbookpages.com)

News of the arrival of 37 agents had not taken long to leak to the general population of the camp and soon emaciated camp inmates were lining the perimeter fence to get a look at the new arrivals. The look of these poor unfortunates further reinforced the belief that the future was bleak for the men; the only inmates who had any resemblance to a picture of health were the Kapos and those with influential roles such as the Lagerschutz. Yeo-Thomas called a meeting of the men to discuss their immediate situation and any future plans.

Despite the negativity from certain of their number it was decided to form an escape committee. The first logical step was to complete a full survey of the camp and security. They received immediate help from two sources, Pertschuk and another F section officer Christopher Burney. Burney was a Lieutenant of Royal Marine Commandos, recruited to SOE he was blind dropped into France to join mission Autogyro, but saw that the mission was compromised and narrowly escaped the clutches of the Gestapo. He set to forming an alternative group but was betrayed and captured in August 1942 and spent the next 18 months locked in solitary confinement at Fresnes before being sent to Buchenwald. He subsequently survived the war and was instrumental in the building of the United Nations headquarters in New York.

Help at this stage was confined to advice as to how best to conduct themselves, as they would get no help from the communist administration, who believed the most outrageous propaganda about the British and especially the British ruling class of which officers would be seen to be of that ilk. They would also view the presence of any organisational expertise as a threat to their dominance of the administration, after all they had wrested the role from the clutches of the greens, (a reference to the green badged criminal inmates), by virtue of their greater ability to organise. The men's new celebrity status was exploited by some; cigarettes were given by some of the Kapos.

DEFIANCE

As part of their isolation the men were exempt from the apel or roll call parades, instead being required to form up outside block 17 to be counted. They were also not placed on work kommandos and food was brought to them. This first day was spent exploring their immediate environment outside the block, as they were not allowed inside until the evening time and then they were able to establish themselves in bedding facilities and the living quarters. One surprise to them was that their rations were slightly superior to that which they experienced at Fresnes but still below that required to keep good health, in this type of low subsistence existence; however, the smallest things meant the difference between survival and death.

That first night Desmond and Yeo-Thomas huddled together in their shared bunk and slept beneath a dirty worn blanket and whilst they were sleeping the SS executed Ernst Thälmann, a former member of the Reichstag and chairman of the German Communist Party. As the Third Reich was crumbling the process of eliminating its enemies was in progress.

Being exempt from the 4 a.m. apel meant the men did not have to rise until 6 a.m. and during these first few days were reliant on news from Pertschuk and Burney until a Dutch Naval officer Pieter Kool was able to obtain permission for them to move about the camp more freely. Pieter Kool is also mentioned in the files of Operation Outreach (HS6/372) and is described as a brave officer who in the 'moral wilderness' of Buchenwald was always available to help others. The Dutch prisoners had not formed the usual racially biased cliques and were highly spoken about by other prisoners. The dreadful conditions of the camp had meant that prisoners were forced to seek the companionship of their fellow countrymen and inter racial dislikes were prevalent. The Russians hated the French as did the Germans, inmates and guards alike. The Polish with very good reason hated the Russians and everyone hated the Czechs. These racial divisions suited the SS who were reliant on a divide and conquer approach to running the camp which all went towards saving valuable manpower resources.

Under the leadership of Yeo-Thomas, closely supported by Desmond, a daily regime was instituted and as best as they could they kept themselves and their clothes clean. Regular exercise was organised and if sent anywhere they formed together and marched under the leadership of one of the more senior officers, such as Desmond. These activities were resisted by some, but eventually they fell into step and found the value of showing the SS that they were first and foremost an undefeated and unrepentant enemy.

After a few days they were able to collect a few of their treasured possessions not looted from them by the train guards, but taken from them on admission to the camp. These possessions included some toiletries and a razor and Desmond was able to retrieve his chess set. On the occasions they were allowed into barracks, chess tournaments and bridge drives were held with the use of Desmond's chess set and a set of cards made by Lieutenant Frank Pickersgill. These items and the games the men played with them had the effect of building their morale, as did the sense of solidarity formed from the shared experience of horror and the therapy of marching and exercise. This raised mental attitude generated further thoughts of escape.

With the ability to move about the camp more freely a further exploration of the camp was made with the discovery of the Kleine Lager or Little Camp. They were horrified by the sight of the ramshackle collection of makeshift huts and tents, where in excess of 30,000 prisoners, mainly Jews were housed. The numbers had been recently swollen by an influx of prisoners from other camps evacuated to Buchenwald ahead of the Russian advances on the Eastern front. Conditions were appalling with insufficient accommodation, poor rations and water supply. Another discovery was a separate enclosure where the Russian POWs were kept. There were about 800 prisoners including eight full Colonels and many junior officers who preferred to be counted as other ranks. These soldiers had sufficient self-discipline and pride to earn the respect of Desmond and his comrades and although they kept themselves to themselves they showed a friendship which was well received.

Surveys of the camp had revealed the perimeter security to be complete with fences, miradors containing guards, machine guns and search lights. The fences were electrically charged and guards made permanent rolling patrols outside the wire, the likelihood of escape was extremely remote. Desmond with Yeo-Thomas and Kane determined to make contact with the camp's administrators to explore the possibility of escape by means of help from within.

Two further F section prisoners came forward to offer their assistance, brothers Alfred and Henry Newton. The brothers had parachuted into France in June 1942 and had been arrested in April 1943; they had also suffered at the hands of the Butcher of Lyon, Klaus Barbie. In separate blocks in Buchenwald both had risen to the position of Stubdiensts and were in a position to offer advice and provide a few luxury items much appreciated by the men. They also made contact with Dr Alfred Balachowsky who was arrested whilst operating as an agent of the SOE Prosper Circuit of Paris. Balachowsky worked at the Pasteur Institute in the field of disease control. In Buchenwald his talents had been put to good use in block 50, a laboratory researching diseases such as typhus and block 46 where prisoners were experimented on with such diseases. Balachowsky was to become a saviour for some prisoners, but too late unfortunately for Desmond.

The trio eventually made contact with camp seniors and the barbershop Kapo, with a view to forming a camp resistance movement, arming themselves and possibly breaking out. These men were the communist nucleus of the camp prisoner administrators and despite the warnings they had been given, the objective was to gain their trust and co-operation. The meetings were polite but fruitless leaving Desmond with the impression that they were viewed as capitalists and therefore deserved whatever fate awaited them. Further discussions with Polish prisoners and the two senior Russian Colonels provided important intelligence and an agreement was made to combine forces and create a system of military units under joint overall command. The units of 10 men were to be placed under the supervision of an officer or competent NCO. It had come to the knowledge of the group that there were stolen arms and ammunition hidden in the camp and that the holders were waiting for the right time to issue orders for insurrection and liberate the camp. Before anything further could be achieved the two Russian Colonels were executed by the SS, no doubt betrayed by their own communist countrymen administrators.

ARRIVAL OF AIRCREW

On 20th August 1944 the 168 aircrew prisoners under the leadership of Squadron Leader Lamason RNZAF arrived at the camp, Their five day train journey had not been interrupted by an air raid as had Desmond's, but they arrived in poor condition. The only food and sustenance they had been given was from the French Red Cross. They had been kept locked up all of the time with one short period off the train per day. On arrival at Buchenwald they also had been designated for execution, classified as Terrorfliegers. They were placed in the little camp and kept in the open. They were shaved; clothing taken from them and replaced with a thin shirt and trousers, but no footwear was issued. They were kept in the open for two weeks on hard stones, through all weathers and given no blankets. Sustenance provided included at 4.30 a.m. a cup of thin soup or coffee, at 7 a.m. a third of a quarter of a loaf of bread and a small portion of margarine, 11 a.m. one cup of black coffee and at 4 p.m. one litre of soup. On every second day each man was given a small piece of sausage and once a week a small portion of jam or honey. In these first two weeks the fliers were made to attend three appels per day and usually lasting six to seven hours in total. Fleas were a problem and the men suffered huge sores for which no medical facilities given. A form, that the guards purported to be from the Red Cross, was circulated asking for such details as to which squadron they were from, numbers and locations. The threat was made that if the form was not completed the men would remain at Buchenwald as terrorists. Some completed the form others did not, but it made no difference and the treatment remained the same. At the end of September one of their number, Flying Officer P.D. Hemmings died of acute rheumatic fever.

Contact was made with these fliers by Yeo-Thomas's escape committee with a rather hair-brained plan to break out of the camp and steal aeroplanes from a nearby airfield and fly to allied lines. This plan was more the fantasy of desperate men rather than a realistic proposition, but at least the liaison resulted in some 40 blankets being scrounged and a note being smuggled from the camp and passed to the local Luftwaffe camp, with the result of two senior Luftwaffe officers attending Buchenwald and demanding the fliers be released to their custody. Eventually all the men were relocated to Stalag Luft III and survived the war.

One other diversion which Desmond and some of the others took advantage of, was to have their portraits sketched by a French prisoner, Auguste Favier. Favier subsequently published his pictorial record of life in Buchenwald and the picture of Desmond featured in the post war published version of the diary of Marguerite Fontaine.

Yeo-Thomas later wrote, "*Hubble, Kane (Keun) and I became inseparable; we shared the same ideals, we were all three determined not to let the Huns get us down. We intended, in spite of*

Sketch of Desmond dated 9.9.44. (Picture Mrs J. Isaac)

being prisoners, to fight to the bitter end. We resolved to do everything in our power to boost the morale of those around us, to remain cheerful and stick together. We were a truly happy trio, enjoying little jokes, reminiscing, sharing everything. Hubble would talk about his children, his family; Kane (Keun) talked of his school, his father, his friends; I did likewise. We discussed the relative merits of such and such restaurant in London, discussed plays we had seen, films, etc. It seemed as though we had formed a friendship that would hold us together, after the war was over, until we died". It certainly lasted unto death.

AIR RAID

On the afternoon of the 24th August 1944 the USAF made a bombing raid with the primary target being the factories on the outside of the camp. The raid caused extensive damage to the Gustloff factory and the Deutsche Ausrüstungs Werke, but as the workers tried to seek shelter the SS guards shot anyone trying to run away. 300 prisoners were killed and many more injured. A few stray bombs hit the camp and the only serious damage was to an SS barracks, where 80 SS personnel were killed. Perhaps the most significant damage caused was to Goethe's Tree, an oak situated near to the laundry building which was hit and killed. Johann Wolfgang von Goethe was a famous German writer/poet who would sit under this tree in reflection. It was a popular myth that the destruction of this oak would signal the fall of Germany. The raid and the destruction of the tree gave a huge lift to the prisoners' spirits who chose to believe that the myth was becoming reality and that their day of liberation was close to hand. For some this would be true!

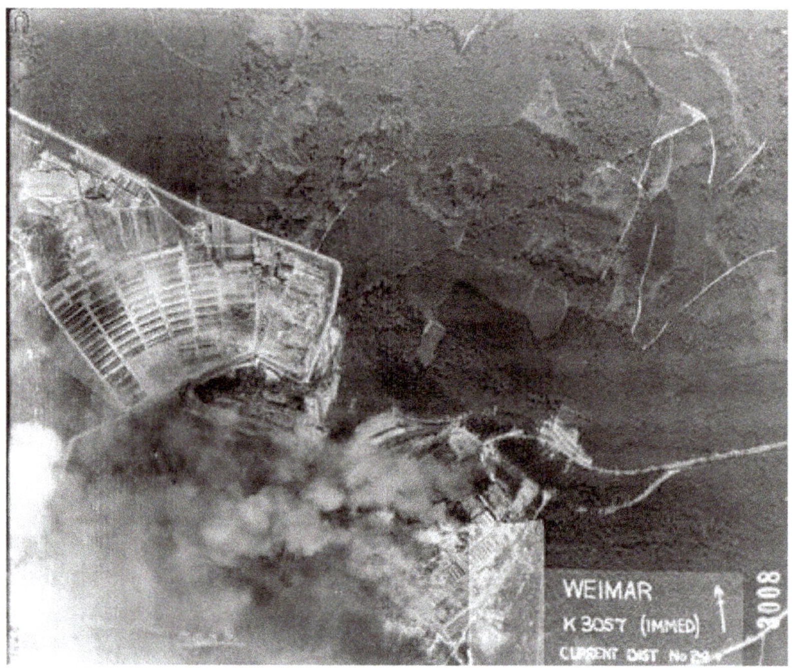

Aerial photograph of bombing raid at Buchenwald.
(Picture scrapbookpages.com)

JOURNEY'S END

On Saturday 9th September 1944 at about 1.30 p.m. the camp loudspeaker system made an announcement ordering 16 of the prisoners to report to the main gate. The names called were; Hubble, Kane, Benoist, Defendini, Allard, Mackenzie, Garel, Garry, Detal, Leccia, Steele, Pickersgill, Mayer, Macalister, Rechenmann and Geelen. None of the men suspected anything sinister as, after all, if they were to be killed, why not back in Paris or on arrival at the camp? They assumed they were required for an examination or some other administrative purpose and after a few words with their remaining friends the men formed up and marched off in the direction of the main gate. On arrival at the gate the 16 men were placed in the punishment cells situated to the right of the main gate and systematically beaten. They were detained at this location for the rest of the day and were not seen until the following day when they were outside the block being exercised. The next day, 10th September 1944 at 5.30 p.m. all 16 men received a further beating and were then taken to the crematorium building where they were executed. They were hung, one by one, from meat hooks in the execution room below the furnace floor. Each man had a noose of rope placed around his neck and made to stand on a small stool, which was then kicked away. It was later reported back to the surviving agents that death was caused by slow strangulation, with each man taking between five to ten minutes each to die. Dr Balachowsky saw the bodies of the 16 and also found a small notebook belonging to Desmond which had slipped from his pocket when he had been hung. He reported this devastating news to Yeo-Thomas and also passed on Desmond's notebook to him. Desmond's corpse and the bodies of the other murdered men were sent up in the lift and burnt in the furnaces that same day. In typical Nazi efficiency the camp record list of names was amended with a red line through the name of each man murdered.

The news came as a huge blow to the other prisoners; some believed that they were to be spared, some lost hope. The men's

Furnaces in the Crematorium. (Photo Mr J. Isaac)

Execution Room beneath the Crematorium.
(Photo Mrs J. Isaac)

possessions were shared amongst the survivors and Yeo-Thomas took Desmond's treasured chess set, which he vowed to take back to England to give to his children. This promise was eventually kept and with some letters and the notebook, the chess set found its way back to the possession of Desmond's family. The notebook and letters were given to SOE sources and are mentioned in Desmond's file, the letters are still in the family's possession and the chess set was subsequently given by one of Desmond's sons to the Imperial War Museum, where it is displayed with Yeo-Thomas's medals in the VC/George Cross room. Unfortunately there is no sign of what happened to the diary, if it had contained any useful information to the Germans it would have been retained by the Gestapo. I believe it is where Desmond made a list of the names of the 37 agents and if so, would have been seen to contain information too sensitive to return to the family.

PART IX

AFTERMATH AND CONCLUSIONS

The post war world became a very different place and it is difficult to find anywhere that does not show signs of this conflict. 55 million people lost their lives, of which nearly 28 million were Russian and six million victims of the Holocaust. Europe was divided into two, east and west and wherever the conflict occurred, the cemeteries reflect the loss. In Britain there are headstones for people from both sides and many nations, crashed German aircrew, naval personnel, victims of aerial bombing and soldiers of nations occupied by Germany, who fought for their countries freedom, but were never able to return. In Poland the memorials refer to the conflict of 1939 only and of Hitlerovsky. There is no mention that the country was then occupied by Stalin's Russia, but the people speak to this day with equal venom of both occupiers. All over France the scars of this conflict are evident, Normandy is a living museum to the invasion, whilst the cemeteries and memorials are a reminder of the cost of occupation from 1940-1945. Soldiers, airmen, sailors, civilians, men and women deported to the labour camps of the Reich, Oradour-sur-Glane a town destroyed and its 642 occupants, men, women and children all murdered in one savage day of reprisal for the loss of one German soldier, with the town left to stand as a memorial to the dead and a reminder of the senselessness of war.

Britain and France started the process of dismantling their colonial empires, as per the agreement made during the formation of the United Nations in 1945 and piece by piece the countries of Africa, India and the Far East were given independence.

BUCHENWALD

Following the murder of Desmond and his fellow agents, more orders for execution arrived and of the remaining agents only six survived the war. Three of them, Yeo-Thomas, Harry Peuleve and Stephane Hessel made a miraculous escape from Buchenwald, with the help of Dr Alfred Balachowsky, who arranged for them to be injected with drugs giving the symptoms of typhus. They were then held in the isolation unit where prisoners were experimented on until three suitable French typhus sufferers died and they were able to change identities with the dead men. The other three hid in the camp until liberation. The full story of Yeo-Thomas is told in the book, 'Bravest of the Brave' by Mark Seaman. Post war he was awarded the George Cross for his exploits as an SOE operative. Buchenwald was finally liberated by American forces on 8th April 1945, but had been partially evacuated by the guards on 4th April. Those inmates left behind rose up and used the hidden weapons to fight the remaining guards. The survivors fought for the recognition that they had liberated themselves, wanting history to reflect their resistance. From 1945 to 1950 the camp was used by the Soviet occupiers for internment, known as NKVD Special Camp number two. Local inhabitants of Weimar were made by the Americans to walk to the camp and see the horrors that were left behind by the retreating Germans. These people were then subject to many years of occupation and suppression, firstly by the Russians and then the East German Communist Government, until the end of the cold war. The camp is now a memorial site and local people are resentful of the continual reminder of what happened on their doorstep. At the time locals denied knowing what had happened but that is all a matter of opinion and for my money the evidence points to the opposite.

Between 11th April and 14th August 1947 31 members of the camp staff including the last Commandant Hermann Pister, doctors and medical staff, one civilian, the SS and Police leader responsible for Buchenwald and three prisoner functionaries were indicted and tried for war crimes at the site of Dachau Concentration Camp, which was being used as an internment facility. All 31 defendants were found guilty by the American Military Tribunal of crimes varying from murder to mistreatment of prisoners; 22 defendants were sentenced to death and hanged, the rest served terms of imprisonment.

CITRONELLE

Following the attack on the Citronelle camp of those resistants captured, 106 men aged 17 years and over, were kept in the field where they were collected and detained. There they were treated brutally and tortured for information, their hands were restrained behind their backs with wire and they were made to kneel with their foreheads on the ground. They were beaten with wood on various parts of the body, tied to the rear of vehicles and dragged along the ground. Some were shot out of hand if they showed any defiance. The following day on 13th June all the remaining detainees were taken to a location in the forest, where pre-prepared graves had been dug and they were shot into the graves four or five to a hole. The bodies were covered but within a few days troops were sent to remove the victims and re-bury them at a secret location, in a part of the forest known as Le Ravin de L'Ours (Bear Ravine). This location was discovered by local people who recovered them a few at a time and hid them in a barn.

Following liberation of the area by American forces in September, the victims were removed to Revin and given proper burial and due respect. In 1948 a Memorial was inaugurated in Revin and every 13th June since this date a ceremony is held at a memorial at the site of the executions, where due respect is given to the martyrs, Desmond is also included in this touching tribute.

Exhumation of Corpses 1944 (Picture Mr P. LeClerc)

Resistant Organisations and Military Personnel
waiting inspection. (Author Pic)

One of the many open graves excavated and preserved to this day (Author photos)

The survivors of the attack of the 12th June escaped to Belgium where they continued to carry out acts of resistance across the border into the Ardennes. This resulted in thousands of German troops engaged trying to pursue and suppress what they perceived as terrorists. Hitler had been asked what his priorities were in the wake of the Normandy landings, with respect to the activities of the resistance movements and he issued a directive to pursue and suppress resistance as a priority. Inevitably this occupied huge resources all over France, but also resulted in some terrible and brutal reprisals against French civilians, for example Oradour-sur-Glane. The Allied Supreme Commander, General Eisenhower, paid tribute to the resistance and credited them as a large factor in the success of the invasion of Europe.

In the same manner, Desmond's incarceration and murder had a similar effect on the German war effort. Huge resources were diverted from front line duties to the imprisonment, transportation and disposal of resistants above and beyond what is normally required in warfare for the care of POWs. This point is made by Adolf Eichmann during his 1961 trial in Israel. As part of his defence he stated that the Third Reich had paid the ultimate sacrifice by carrying out the Holocaust. The transports and troops that could have been used to reinforce and supply the front lines were diverted to carry civilians to death and labour camps. Whilst his other arguments about not making a profit from the murder of civilians are perverse and untrue, the result of his trial reflected that. The point is that Desmond and many others like him continued to contribute to the allied war effort whilst they lived and were perceived as a threat.

Colonel Bollardière remained in the French military and rose to the rank of General. His exemplary career was blighted by his experience in Algeria when in 1957 he criticised the use of torture. As a result he was sentenced to 60 days detention and then posted to fictitious duties. He resigned from the military and became a pacifist in the 1970s; he died in 1986.

Victor Layton likewise remained in the army as an aeronautical engineer and retired with the rank of Colonel. He then worked as a civil engineer until his retirement. He remained in contact with his French friends of the Ardennes and his final word was a letter read at the inauguration of a memorial to the mission Citronelle in the forest of Manises in June 2010. He died later that year the last surviving member of the mission.

On 27th September1944 George Whitehead stepped out of the forest and made contact with the liberating US troops. This encounter is mentioned in the Military Government Journal for the day and describes him as 'an odd-looking character, his face hidden by a beard and wearing civilian clothes which were worse for wear'. His mission over, the objective was to return military arms and equipment back into the hands of proper authority. The description is worthy of mention to give a picture of the effects of living rough since June. Whitehead returned to civilian life in England and spent many post war years ensuring that all concerned with Citronelle were appropriately recognised by Britain. In Poland his family businesses were confiscated by the communists and his family treated as exploiters of workers. His brother Charles was imprisoned and possessions confiscated.

George died in 1986 and all his papers were consigned to a skip leaving a huge hole in the available records of this exploit.

Capitaine Gerard Brault was demobilised from the army in March 1946 and returned to civilian life. He made a career with import and export companies in various countries. He was made an Officer of the Legion d'honneur, awarded the Croix de Guerre with Palm Vermeil, the Military Medal, the Medal of the Resistance, escapees and the British Military Cross. He died in Cannes in March 2004.

Captain Jacques Chavane remained in the army after the liberation of France and was assigned to the Directorate of Studies and Research and the Inspectorate of Paratroopers. In 1951 he was posted to Colonial Infantry Administration with the High Command in Cameroon and Morocco. He was awarded The Croix de Guerre with Palm 1939-45 and is a knight of the Legion of Honour.

On completion of the mission Lieutenant Lucien Goetghebeur returned to London where he volunteered to serve in the Far East. He went to Calcutta and then to the French Military Mission in China and was demobilised in 1947. He was awarded the Croix de Guerre with Silver Star, British Military Cross, the Medal of Escapees and the Medal of the Resistance.

Lieutenant Gerard Racine left the army in July 1945; he was mentioned in dispatches and awarded the Medal of the Resistance by General de Gaulle.

Colonel Grabowski and Major Molinari survived the war, but were never brought to justice for the atrocities they were responsible for. Grabowski was arrested by British troops in October 1945 but was then released. In April 1951 a French military tribunal found them guilty in absentia of murder and sentenced them to death. Grabowski died in Hanover in July 1964. Molinari continued his career with the Bundeswehr and commanded the 7th Division of Dragoons near Dortmund; he was also an advisor to Chancellor Helmut Kohl. He rose to the rank of Major General but resigned in November 1970 following a scandal based on the events of 1944. He died in December 1993 aged 81.

Following the liberation of the Ardennes area by US troops in September 1944, various people independently set up enquiries into the events in the Manise forest with a view to apportioning blame. There was inevitably a mixture of politics and personal agendas involved and some of the accusations made were in an effort to displace blame for failings onto others. In October 1945 Robert Charton was put on trial, but was acquitted by the court of any wrong doing. As previously mentioned Léon Uhl was tried as a collaborator for telling the Germans the location of the Maquis camp, a fact they already knew from the aerial photographs taken on the morning of the 6th June. Despite his heroic escape and continued fighting until liberation he was convicted and sentenced to two years imprisonment with hard labour, a sure indicator that a sacrificial lamb was required.

LA FERME FONTAINE

The Fontaine family returned to peacetime farming and were justly rewarded for their bravery. The last award was in 2010 when Georgette Fontaine, the last surviving member of the family, was appointed to the Légion d'Honneur for her part in the resistance movement. That same year I had the distinct honour of interviewing her in the farm where she still lives. The house is a time warp and other than routine maintenance and the addition of surface mounted electricity, it is exactly the same as when Desmond was entertained there in 1944.

SOE

By the end of the Second World War SOE had built a vast, almost global organisation of intelligence gathering, contacts, scientific development and agent training. SOE's members expected to be of further use to their country but in the post war political changes, SOE was disbanded and discarded and other than a few agents, the old guard of British intelligence finally prevailed and saw the 'amateur upstart' assigned to the archives of secret files. The commandeered estates were handed back to their owners,

Mme Georgette Fontaine 2010 and Author

Desmond's Jumpsuit and M. P. LeClerc. (Author photo)

stores and equipment disposed of and employees de-mobbed. This left many people in urgent need of employment including Sgt. Peter Wall-Row, the photographer responsible for agent identity pictures and whom Desmond had met at Hackett School. Wall-Row wrote to military records Room 98, Horse Guards in July 1945 asking for the whereabouts of Desmond, presumably seeking employment within the family businesses. The reply was surprisingly prompt and open bearing in mind that matters were still very secretive. Wall-Row eventually returned to his pre-war career with Kodak, had a family, a full and prosperous life and died in 2002.

Many agents felt betrayed and that their contribution was not properly recognised, even though awards for bravery and service had been distributed. The highest award given was the George Cross, as the Victoria Cross had not been deemed appropriate, as the criteria was not met. The administration network had to be unravelled and records stored and many were destroyed leaving large holes in available research for future biographers and historians. At the cessation of hostilities the whereabouts of 118 F section agents were unknown and enquiries commenced to trace their fate and the perpetrators of war crimes. The F section secretary to Maurice Buckmaster, Vera Atkins, was given military rank in the Women's Auxiliary Air force and spent many months tracing the missing men and women; she accounted for the fate of all bar one.

SOE was finally closed down on 15th January 1946. The survivors formed a post war institution to this day known as 'The Special Forces Club'. I was treated to a marvellous luncheon there one day during my research and the walls are covered with photographs of those SOE agents who lost their lives, including Desmond.

AWARDS

Desmond's file shows that he was recommended for an MBE and the citation reads:

"From October 1942 to November 1943 Capt. HUBBLE was principle representative of a combined special mission in WEST AFRICA, where he served in BATHURST and FREETOWN successively. In these posts he displayed a high sense of responsibility, initiative and discretion.

On his return to the U.K. he volunteered to go on a mission to the Maquis in FRANCE and was parachuted to the ARDENNES on 5th June 1944. On 12th June he went out with a reconnaissance party which ran into a German patrol. A skirmish ensued during which HUBBLE was separated with one or two others, and captured. In the short interval between his arrival and capture he had already laid on a number of air operations and provided much information on the area in his cables.

HUBBLE was imprisoned at ST. QUENTON. Then at FRESNES and COMPIEGNE before being sent to BUCHENWALD. He was repeatedly very badly beaten and tortured but all reports from the ARDENNES area, FRESNES and BUCHENWALD, concur in their descriptions of the admirable fortitude with which he faced these trials, and no compromising information was given away by him. He was killed in September 1944.

It is recommended that Captain HUBBLE be awarded a posthumous Mention in Despatches'.

(signed) C Mc. V Gubbins
Major-General
10th Jan '46".

The MBE was denied and returned for the recommendation to be re-issued for a Mention in Despatches which was awarded. He was also awarded the following:

Top: Mention in Despatches certificate signed by the Secretary of State with War medal 1939-45 bearing the Mention in Despatches Oak Leaf

Centre: Médaille de la Reconnaissance française (in silver) Bottom row;

Left: 1939-45 Star. Middle: France and Germany Star.

Right: 1939-45 Defence Medal

Right: Croix de Guerre avec Palm. (War Cross and Bronze Palm awarded to Belgians and Allied military personnel for bravery in the face of the enemy, Mentioned in despatches) Photos Mr Julian Hubble.

Left: Croix de Chevalier de L'Ordre Royal du Lion avec Palm. (Royal Order of the Lion, Knight with gold and silver Palm awarded by Belgium for Distinguished Service in the Congo).

DESMOND'S LEGACY

Desmond's file reflects the difficulties faced by both the authorities and family of personnel lost, with no clear evidence of their fate. Initially messages from Citronelle reported that he had been captured and authority sought to elevate George Whitehead from the status of Administration Officer, to that of full member, in place of Desmond who was not initially posted as missing for reasons of his own security. In recognition of his request for sensitivity, when informing family due to his domestic circumstances, there is an incomplete record of the to-ing and fro-ing of suggestions as to the wording of notice of his fate and of whom to deliver the news to. He was eventually posted as an SOE Battle casualty and from the evidence of Yeo-Thomas and Professor Balachowsky he was posted, missing presumed killed on or after 11th September 1944. The initial draft letter was returned for amendment as it was feared that the wording may give an indication of the secretive nature of his work. The final draft is retained in family records and was delivered as per his request to his mother. Desmond's employment status was changed from 'specially employed' to "entitled" to remuneration from Army funds.

The effects on Desmond's family were complicated by Margaret's medical condition. As mentioned previously, common for the day, she had received electric shock therapy for post-natal depression and this had caused brain damage leaving her incapable of looking after the children. Of Desmond's two sons, Peter was sent to boarding school at Tonbridge, Michael went to Dartmouth Naval Academy and subsequently served as an officer on submarines. Peter also served in the military in the Parachute Regiment, whilst daughter Jacquie was adopted by an aunt and uncle who emigrated to New Zealand. It was not until adulthood and return to Britain that Jacquie was able to re-discover her brothers; however she does value the benefit of an extended family and the diverse experience that living on the other side of the world gives. Parents were robbed of a son, a wife denied the care of her husband and children deprived the right of a father, whilst Britain lost a shining star whose wartime experience would have enhanced his future contribution to the nation. The available life records of those chosen to join SOE show that they largely became successful in whatever venture they applied themselves to after the war.

Desmond's parents, together with his sister and son Michael, attended the 1948 inauguration of the Revin memorial and gave a Union Flag and a framed picture of Desmond to the Fontaine family. The picture still hangs on the dining room wall of the farmhouse, alongside that of President de Gaulle, where Desmond and Citronelle 2 celebrated the invasion with the Fontaine family and other resistants. The flag is still a prized possession of

The Revin Memorial. (Wild boar is the animal of the Ardennes author photo)

Georgette Fontaine as is Desmond's jump suit. Desmond's name was also placed on the memorial in Bayeux, which commemorates those who lost their lives in the Invasion battles.

Desmond's three children eventually grew to be well educated and professional people; they all married and had children of their own. There are now four grandchildren with professions ranging from educators to entrepreneurs and nine great grandchildren a total of 13 direct descendants (2013).

In 1995, Peter who had long grieved for his father summoned the fortitude to go to Buchenwald and visit the place of his father's murder. The Sunday Express of 9th April 1995 told the story in a two page article and described the visit as an extremely emotional experience, but one that gave him some peace of mind. Peter took with him his father's treasured chess set and collected three small pebbles for keepsakes, one for himself and one each for his two siblings.

In 2010 Desmond's daughter Jacquie and other family members attended the memorial service in Revin where Jacquie also laid a wreath for her father on behalf of The Royal British Legion.

Hubble Family members June 13th 2010.
Mrs J. Isaac centre (Author Photo)

That same year Jacquie, husband Keith and son Jamie made the same pilgrimage to Buchenwald as Peter had made in 1995. This was with a tour organised by the Special Forces Club for a memorial to be placed in honour of her father and the other agents who perished. Two large black marble tablets are now wall mounted in the crematorium to honour the dead. Jacquie laid a wreath on behalf of all the children who lost a father and met the last surviving member of the 37, Stephane Hessel, at the time 93 years old. The military representation was General Sir Michael Rose and there were also representatives of numerous organisations including the Royal British Legion. Jacquie described her visit in detail and showed immense fortitude to be able to write a detailed account immediately on her return. I am sure Desmond would be incredibly proud of his legacy.

Whether Desmond's sacrifice was worthwhile is part of a much larger question, was the conflict worth fighting? Anti-war opinionists would argue that Hitler would have died and eventually normality would have returned to Europe. Some Jewish historians are scathing of the Allied lack of effort to prevent or diminish

The memorial at Buchenwald. (Photo Mr J. Isaac)

the Holocaust. Certainly Bomber Command was reluctant to divert resources from the main task of destroying German industry and bringing the nation to its knees in favour of targeting the transport networks being used to deliver victims to the camps. Russian forces chose to delay taking objectives such as Warsaw, which no doubt would have saved Jewish lives. The arguments are endless and very much a personal choice, but the bombing of Buchenwald did not prevent Desmond from being murdered!

Opinion as to whether Desmond should have committed himself is divided, he certainly had a choice. He volunteered for service when he could have been developing his businesses to contribute to the war effort and been classified as involved in essential war work. He was initially assigned to military work, essential to the defence of Britain and could well have sat out the war in a comfortable home posting. His initial assignment to France was no doubt as a volunteer answering the call for speakers of foreign languages and likewise his deployment to Africa, where he could have spent the rest of the war in safety and comfort. A critical comment made about him was that he volunteered to absent himself from a difficult domestic situation; however all the evidence, in my humble opinion, points to the opposite. His formative years were spent in institutions where service and duty was impressed on him and his family ethic is clearly that of hard work and advancement. He had multiple opportunities to spend the war at home or in non-operational comfortable postings away from danger, but chose not to. Desmond had the foresight to predict the danger that Hitler posed and that Britain should be preparing for war. He joined the army the day before war was declared and then volunteered for further services which eventually led to his death. During his service with Citronelle and then his trials of captivity he showed fortitude, courage and leadership skills which earned him the admiration and respect of his peers. He is variously described by those who knew him as courageous, humorous and possessing an endearing personality. Desmond had a choice to look after himself and his own, or place those secondary to his duty to fight an evil which was consuming the world. In my estimation he made the right choice and for that I and millions more have been able to live their lives in freedom.

As for my own connection to Desmond, Paul Serrafique Manise died on 30th May 1940, in time to see his beloved France invaded, but before its great shame. He did not live to see the time his 'old boys' were being either slaughtered, as in Desmond's case, or elevated to fame as per Bernard Law Montgomery. On his passing, French ceased to be used in the Manise household and his son Richard, my grandfather, recorded as 'French by parentage', was faced with a choice and chose to be English. As for my quest to determine my French ancestry, I have yet to determine why there is a forest and a river named Manise; the Ardennes genealogical group believe the word Manise is derived from an ancient French word meaning earth. So much for any desires on my behalf to have blue blood in my veins! On the upside, in the early 19th century one of my descendants, M. Jaque Joseph Manise (B. 24.6.1798) married a lady named Marie-Antoinette, perhaps I should be satisfied with that fact and eat some cake!

SOURCES

INTERVIEWS

Dr. D. Finlay-Maxwell (Major SOE and Royal Signals) (SOE history and codes)

Madame Georgette Fontaine, Une Chevalier de la Legion d'honneur, (Maquis des Manises, Citronelle and Captain Hubble)

Mrs. Jacquie Isaac (nee Hubble) (Family records and photographs)

Mr Jamie Isaac (Photographs Buchenwald)

Mr. Julian Hubble (Maps)

Monsieur Philippe Leclerc (Citronelle, French Archives and Photographs)

Ms Virginia McKenna (Photographs and details)

NATIONAL ARCHIVES FILES

HS9/756/1 (Hubble pf)

HS6/356 (Citronelle)

WO106/4994 (Swayne)

WO 311/1015 (Fresnes to Buchenwald)

HS 6/372 (Operation Outhall)

HS 9/78/11 (Balachowsky)

WO311/83 (War crimes Manises)

War Cabinet Records

WO/252 McKenzie

WO/311 War Crimes

WO106/4994 Swayne

RESOURCES

A Life in Secrets; Vera Atkins and the Lost Agents, Sarah Helm

Beaulieu; Finishing School for Secret Agents

Belgium and the Congo; 1885-1980, Guy Vanthemsche

Bravest of the Brave and information re George Whitehead; Mr Mark Seaman

Exmoor in Wartime 1939-1945; Jack Hurley

Le Maquis Des Manises Revin

Les Vieux Moulins de Thilay Haut Lieu De La Resistance Ardennaise; Journal de Marguerite Fontaine

Public Records; Births deaths and marriages

RAF Tempsford, Churchill's Most Secret Airfield; Bernard O'Connor

SOE a New Instrument of War, Various authors; Editor Mark Seaman

SOE 1940-1946; Professor M.R.D. Foot

SOE: The Scientific Secrets; F. Boyce and D. Everett

Soldiers, Airmen, Spies and Whisperers; Professor Nancy Ellen Lawler

Special Forces in the Invasion of France; Paul Gaujac

Spirit of Resistance: The Life of Harry Peuleve; Nigel Perrin

Survivor of Buchenwald: My Personal Odyssey Through Hell; Louis Gros

The Beasts of Buchenwald: Karl & Ilse Koch; Flint Whitlock

The British Empire & the Second World War; Ashley Jackson

The Secret History of SOE, 1940-45; Professor William Mackenzie

Tonbridge School records. Mrs Beverley Mathews, Senior Librarian

War and the 20th Century; Christopher Coker

Letter to Mr Michael Elcock; Professor M.R.D. Foot

Convoy Peewit: August 8, 1940 The first day of the Battle of Britain; Andy Saunders

GLOSSARY OF TERMS AND ABBREVIATIONS

Apel	Roll call in Concentration Camps
Anschluss	German for Connection or Union
BCRA	Bureau Central de Renseignements et d'Action
BEF	British Expeditionary Force
Blitz Kreig	German, Lightening War
Blockältester	Block elder or leader prisoner position in concentration camp
Chevalier de la Légion d'honneur	French award, Knight of the Legion of Honour
Croix de Guerre avec Palme	French award, War Cross with Palm
DFC & Bar	Distinguished Flying Cross (Bar signifies awarded a second time)
Effektenkammer	Prisoners possessions store
Einsatzgruppen	Murder squads employed on the Eastern front.
F Section	French section dealing with non-Gaullist resistance
Feldgendarmerie	Military police SS or Wehrmacht
Feldkomandantur 684	German Military command responsible for the Ardennes area
GAF	German Air Force (Luftwaffe)
GSO	General Staff Officer
Kapo	Concentration Camp inmate in charge of other prisoners
Work Kommando	Term used to describe a work detail in a Concentration Camp
Konzentrationslager.	Concentration Camp

Lagerälteste	Concentration camp elder, prisoner in charge of all departments run by other prisoners
Lagerschutz	Inmate trustee/police
Luftwaffe	German air force
M.	Monsieur (Mr)
Mme.	Madame (Mrs)
Mlle.	Mademoiselle (Miss)
Maquis	Bush or Shrub (used to describe rural groups of resistants)
MEW	Ministry of Economic Warfare
Maquisards	Members of a Maquis
MC	Military Cross
Miradors	Concentration Camp watchtowers
MTB	Motor Torpedo Boat
NCO	Non Commissioned Officer
OSS	Office of Strategic Service. (US equivalent of SOE forerunner to the CIA)
OTC	Officer Training Corps
Pf	Personal File
POW	Prisoner of War
PWE	Political Warfare Executive
RAF	Royal Air Force
RAFVR	Royal Air Force Volunteer Reserve
RNZAF	Royal New Zealand Air Force
RF Section	French section dealing with De Gaulle loyalists
SD	Sicherheitsdienst (SS Intelligence agency)
SHAEF	Supreme Headquarters Allied Expeditionary Force
SIS	Secret Intelligence Service
SOE	Special Operations Executive
Sous-lieutenant	Sub-Lieutenant or second lieutenant
SS	Schutzstaffel (bodyguard and state police)
SS-Totenkopfverbände	Deaths head units responsible for administration of camps
Straflager	Disciplinary or punishment camp
STS	SOE Special Training School
Stubdiensts	Assistants to Blockältesters
Terrorfliegers	Terror Flyers (German description of bomber or SOE support aircrews)

TR	Travaux Ruraux (French military counter-intelligence service)
Vichy	Town where the unoccupied part of France was governed from
Wermacht	German army
WO	War Office
W Section	West African section of SOE
WT	Wireless Telegraph

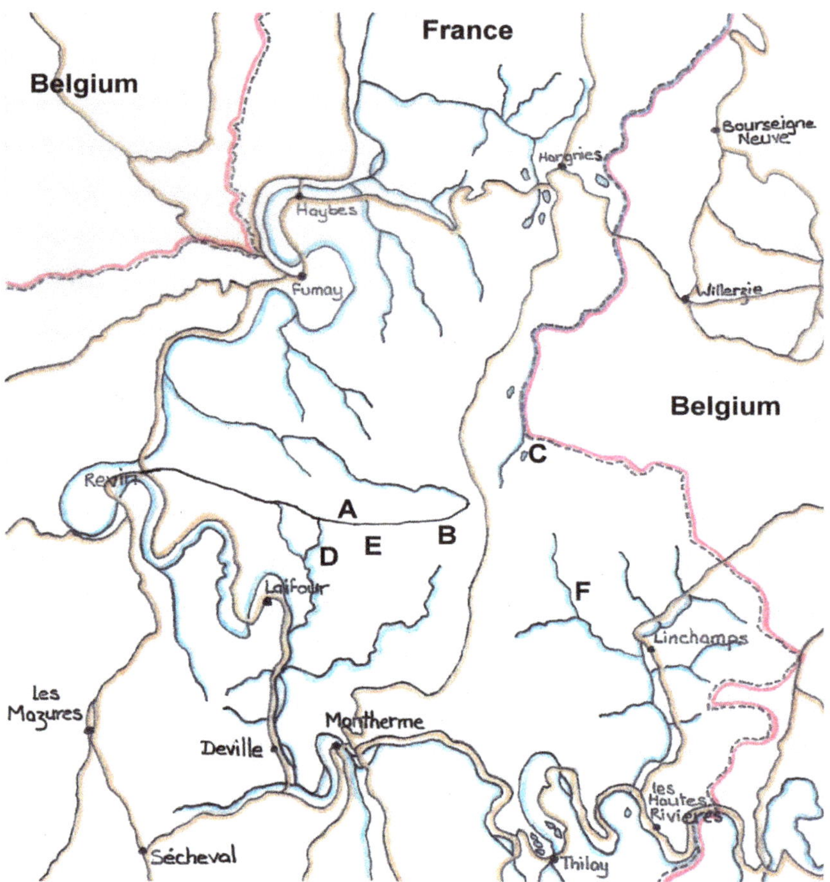

Key;

Red line with dotted black = French/Belgian Border

Black and brown lines = Roads

Blue and black lines = Rivers

A = Maquis du Manises Camp B = Les Vieux Moulins d' Hargnies (Field where prisoners held) C = Parachute drop site Astrologie D = German camp

E = Site of executions F = Bear Ravine

ABOUT THE AUTHOR

Mick is a retired British police officer having served in both Birmingham City and West Midlands forces. He served in both uniform, CID and other specialist units gaining experience and expertise in major investigation. In retirement he has combined two life long passions, motorcycling and history, resulting in research trips throughout Western Europe and books about the two World Wars.

A member and supporter of the Royal British Legion, profits from this book will be donated to that worthy cause.